USDA

United States
Department of
Agriculture

Forest Service

**Northern
Research Station**

General Technical
Report NRS-33

# Prescribing Regeneration Treatments for Mixed-Oak Forests in the Mid-Atlantic Region

## Abstract

Includes guidelines for using the SILVAH decision-support system to perpetuate oak forests in the Mid-Atlantic region. Six chapters provide information on values of oak forests, inventory methods, key decision variables, decision charts, and silvicultural prescriptions, as well as guidance on fostering young stands. Sample tally sheets and SILVAH computer printouts are included in the Appendix.

Manuscript received for publication 17 April 2008

# Prescribing Regeneration Treatments for Mixed Oak Forests in the Mid-Atlantic Region

## General Technical Report NRS-33

**Patrick H. Brose**
**Kurt W. Gottschalk**
**Stephen B. Horsley**
**Peter D. Knopp**
**James N. Kochenderfer**
**Barbara J. McGuinness**
**Gary W. Miller**
**Todd E. Ristau**
**Scott H. Stoleson**
**Susan L. Stout**

---

### About the Authors

PATRICK H. BROSE is a research forester with the U.S. Forest Service's Northern Research Station at Irvine, Pennsylvania.

KURT W. GOTTSCHALK is a research forester and the project leader with the Northern Research Station at Morgantown, West Virginia.

STEVEN B. HORSLEY is a research plant physiologist and emeritus scientist with the Northern Research Station at Irvine, Pennsylvania.

PETER D. KNOPP is a computer specialist with the Northern Research Station at Delaware, Ohio.

JAMES N. KOCHENDERFER is a research forester and emeritus scientist with the Northern Research Station at Parsons, West Virginia.

BARBARA J. MCGUINNESS is an environmental literacy coordinator with the Northern Research Station at Irvine, Pennsylvania.

GARY W. MILLER is a research forester with the Northern Research Station at Morgantown, West Virginia.

TODD E. RISTAU is a research ecologist with the Northern Research Station at Irvine, Pennsylvania.

SCOTT H. STOLESON is a research wildlife biologist with the Northern Research Station at Irvine, Pennsylvania.

SUSAN L. STOUT is a research forester and the project leader with the Northern Research Station at Irvine, Pennsylvania.

# CONTENTS

Figure 1.1.—The five states of the
mid-Atlantic region of the eastern United States.

# CHAPTER 1: INTRODUCTION

Patrick Brose, Kurt Gottschalk, Gary Miller, Scott Stoleson, and Susan Stout

The mixed-oak (*Quercus* spp.) forest is one of the major forest types of the mid-Atlantic region: Delaware, Maryland, New Jersey, Pennsylvania, and West Virginia (Fig.1.1). Twenty-one oak species grow in this region but five species predominate (97 percent of total oak volume); northern red (*Q. rubra*), chestnut (*Q. montana*), white (*Q. alba*), black (*Q. velutina*), and scarlet (*Q. coccinea*). Currently, mixed-oak forests occupy 19.4 million of the 32.4 million acres of forest land in this region (Widmann and McWilliams 2006).

Despite this widespread dominance, mixed-oak forests are in decline and require careful management to be sustained. Throughout much of the mid-Atlantic region, oaks are being replaced by other hardwood species. Recent U.S. Forest Service, Forest Inventory and Analysis (FIA) data show that oak accounts for 29 percent of the total growing-stock volume in the region but also 43 percent of the removals (Widmann and McWilliams 2006). In Pennsylvania, other FIA data show that for all stems larger than 2 inches in diameter at breast height (d.b.h.), red maple (*Acer rubrum*) and black birch (*Betula lenta*) are the two most common species and the most common oak, northern red, is the ninth most abundant hardwood (McWilliams and others 2004). The disparity is evident in the sapling and pole size classes where red maple

1

outnumbers all oaks by ratios of 6:1 and 3:1, respectively. As mature oaks are harvested or succumb to various causes, they are being replaced by hardwood species other than oaks.

Why is this change occurring? Is it desirable or undesirable? What can be done about it? The objectives of this chapter are to briefly explain the driving forces behind this forest-type conversion, the values of oak forests, describe the oak regeneration problem, and provide an introduction to the SILVAH decision-support system.

## Changing Disturbance Regimes

Oak forests often are referred to as a disturbance-mediated climax forest or disclimax (Nowacki and Abrams 1992, Rentch and Hicks 2005). After the end of the last glacial period about 12,000 years ago, oak species gradually migrated northward from their southern refuge. For the most part, the oak forests of the mid-Atlantic region have been in place for the last 6,000 to 8,000 years (Patterson 2006). The continued dominance through those millennia was due to an inherent compatibility between the silvics of the oak species and the disturbance regime of that era. That regime was periodic surface fires coupled with occasional canopy-level disturbances (Abrams 2003, Brose and others 2001, Whitney and DeCant 2003). The fires were primarily the product of American Indian cultural activities as they burned the forests for numerous reasons (Denevan 1992). Lightning also contributed to fires (Cohen and Dellinger 2006, Cohen and others 2007, Ruffner and Abrams 1998).

The oaks are well adapted to survive and thrive in a periodic surface fire regime. The bark on mature oaks is thick, allowing them to easily withstand surface fires that injure or kill thin-barked competitors. When injured, oaks quickly compartmentalize the wound and because most oaks are long lived; therefore they simply outlast many of the competitors in a periodic fire regime. Oak regeneration quickly develops large, deep roots when conditions are suitable. Such roots allow large seedling and sapling oaks to sprout after being topkilled by fire. Some competitors lack this trait, or it is poorly developed, and few other species are as the oaks in sprouting repeatedly.

Canopy disturbances before European stettlement came from a variety of sources (Brose and Waldrop 2006, Rentch and Hicks 2005). The most common likely were small gaps that formed when a lightning strike killed an individual tree or a thunderstorm microburst felled several trees. Other canopy disturbances, e.g., an insect outbreak or passenger pigeon (*Ectopistes migratorius*) activity, occurred less often but on a larger scale, possibly at the stand level (Ellsworth and McComb 2003). Landscape-level canopy disturbances probably were the least common but largest and included hurricanes, ice storms, and tornadoes.

These two types of disturbances—periodic surface fires and canopy-level openings—worked together to perpetuate oak forests (Fig. 1.2). The fires removed thin-barked, non-oak competitors and maintained a moderate understory light level that promoted the development of oak regeneration with large roots. When a gap formed, the oak regeneration beneath it was well positioned to grow rapidly into the canopy. So long as fires and canopy gaps occurred on an intermittent basis, oak forests were sustained and did so for millennia.

Figure 1.2.—Historically, mixed-oak forests were maintained through a combination of periodic canopy-level disturbances and surface fires.

The fire regime fluctuated wildly from the mid-1800s to the early 1900s (Brose and others 2001). First, fire frequency and intensity greatly increased as the eastern forests were cut heavily and repeatedly to meet the demand of a growing population amid the Industrial Revolution. By the early 20th century, these intense fires were so problematic that they led to a public forest policy of fire exclusion throughout the mid-Atlantic region. Within several decades, fire occurrence and acreage burned were almost nonexistent (Abrams and Nowacki 1992). Fire became ecologically extinct. It no longer filled its role of minimizing the occurrence of thin-barked, shade-tolerant hardwood species such as American beech (*Fagus grandifolia*), red maple, and sugar maple (*A. saccharum*) in the understories of oak forests. In the absence of fire, these species formed dense midstory canopies that reduced understory light to the point that oak regeneration died or could not develop roots to a competitive size. Consequently, when a canopy gap occurred, it was filled by beech or maple instead of an oak. Fire also limited the occurrence of fast-growing, shade-intolerant hardwood species such as black cherry (*Prunus serotina*), black birch, and yellow-poplar (*Liriodendron tulipifera*) that could invade and capture canopy gaps.

Exclusion of fire was not the only change introduced to the oak forests that had negative consequences. Chestnut blight (*Cryphonectria parasitica*) killed the American chestnut (*Castanea dentata*) and in doing so removed a reliable mast producer from the forest. Wildlife accustomed to feeding on chestnuts shifted to acorns, likely reducing the proportion of seed crops that germinated successfully. White-tailed deer (*Odocoileus virginianus*), nearly extirpated by unregulated market hunting, were reintroduced into a forest landscape devoid of most predators. Subsequent game laws encouraged the rapid expansion of the deer herd, which not only consumed acorns, but also preferentially browsed oak seedlings while avoiding less palatable species e.g., black cherry.

More recently, exotic pests, such as gypsy moth (*Lymantria dispar*) that preferentially defoliate oaks, spread throughout the region. Periodic outbreaks of this pest further reduced the frequency and size of acorn crops. Also, timber harvesting often was concentrated on the most valuable species (high-grading) with little or no regard to the conditions for regeneration. This new disturbance regime (no fire, chronic deer browsing, more frequent canopy disturbances that target oaks) has come about so rapidly that oaks have not had time to adapt to it through natural selection. Consequently, the oak forests are changing to species mixes with much less oak.

## The Values of Oak Forests

This shift in species composition in mixed-oak forests is often undesirable to natural resource professionals and society as a whole because oaks have both ecological and economic value (Smith 2006). Throughout the mid-Atlantic region, oaks grow on a variety of sites: from chestnut oak on xeric ridges to northern red oak on mesic lower slopes (Fig. 1.3). Oaks are long lived, quite resistant to rot, and grow to large sizes. These characteristics indicate that, once established, oak forests are relatively stable plant communities (Smith 2006). Once they achieve canopy dominance, oaks likely will persist for decades to centuries as they readily withstand insect outbreaks, lightning strikes, wind events, and ice storms. When damage does occur, the ability to compartmentalize rot helps ensure their continued survival (Shigo 1984). Injury sites may become cavities which, in turn, become dens for wildlife. Dens are especially valuable as wildlife habitat when they occur in large trees (Godfrey and others 2000).

Photo by Patrick Brose, Northern Research Station

Figure 1.3.—Mixed-oak forests are found on diverse sites ranging from rich valley floors to dry ridges.

Canopies of oak forests are penetrated easily by sunlight; this allows the development of diverse herbaceous and shrub communities (Fralish 2004). Oaks produce copious amounts of foliage that is slow to decompose (Loomis 1974, 1975). In upland settings, this leaf litter is an excellent fuel source for low-intensity surface fires, an ecological process that further diversifies forest-floor plant communities (Hutchinson 2006). In aquatic environments, oak leaves are a valuable source of detritus that directly and indirectly benefits numerous organisms (Rubbo and Kiesecker 2004).

Oaks are well known for producing acorns. Relatively large, readily digestible, easily stored, and high in nutrition, acorns are a valuable food resource for many animals (Kirkpatrick and Pekins 2002, McShea and Healy 2002). Within the mid-Atlantic region, more than 50 vertebrate species regularly consume acorns, among them many important game animals such as white-tailed deer, black bear (*Ursus americanus*), tree squirrels (*Sciurus* spp.), wild turkey (*Meleagris gallopavo*), wood ducks (*Aix sponsa*), and ruffed grouse (*Bonasa umbellus*). Acorns also constitute a major portion of the diets of nongame species as diverse as red-headed woodpeckers (*Melanerpes erythrocephalus*), blue jays (*Cyanocitta cristata*), white-footed mice (*Peromyscus leucopus*), and chipmunks (*Tamias striatus*). Since the loss of the American chestnut, acorns are the primary source of hard mast in the region.

Many species of wildlife in oak forests depend on acorns to such an extent that they exhibit physiological and population responses to fluctuations in acorn crops. For example, acorn availability can affect the weight, condition, reproductive rates, and antler characteristics of white-tailed deer (Wentworth and others 1992). Similarly, rates of birth, survival, and dispersal in black bear vary with the abundance and distribution of acorn crops (Pelton 1989). Variation in mast production also influences population levels and distributions of a variety of small mammals and birds, including mice, squirrels, jays, and woodpeckers (McShea 2000, Rodewald 2003).

Oaks provide other valuable resources to wildlife in addition to mast. In comparing bird densities among mature stands dominated by oak or by red maple, Rodewald and Abrams (2002) found that oaks supported a significantly higher abundance of birds in all seasons. Avian species richness was significantly greater in oak than in maple stands (Fig. 1.4). Differences were greatest in autumn during masting and in spring when oak flowers attract insects. They predicted that a conversion of oak forests to red maple would have a severe impact on bird communities in the Eastern United States.

Figure 1.4.—The cerulean warbler is one of the neotropical migrant species that relies almost exclusively on mixed-oak forests. It generally avoids maple-dominated forests.

Oak species are of great economic importance to the mid-Atlantic region. According to the quarterly "Timber Market Report" (Jacobson and Finley 2007), northern red oak was the second most valuable tree species in Pennsylvania from 1992 to 2005 (Fig. 1.5). Its stumpage price was exceeded only by that of black cherry. During that same period, the stumpage price for the other oaks consistently ranked fourth among all commercial species. Oak saw logs are used for a variety of products ranging from cabinets, fine furniture, flooring, and whiskey barrels to dimension lumber, pallets, and railroad ties. The wood-products industries employ thousands of people in the region, a significant proportion of which is related to the growth, harvest, manufacturing, and delivery of products from oak species.

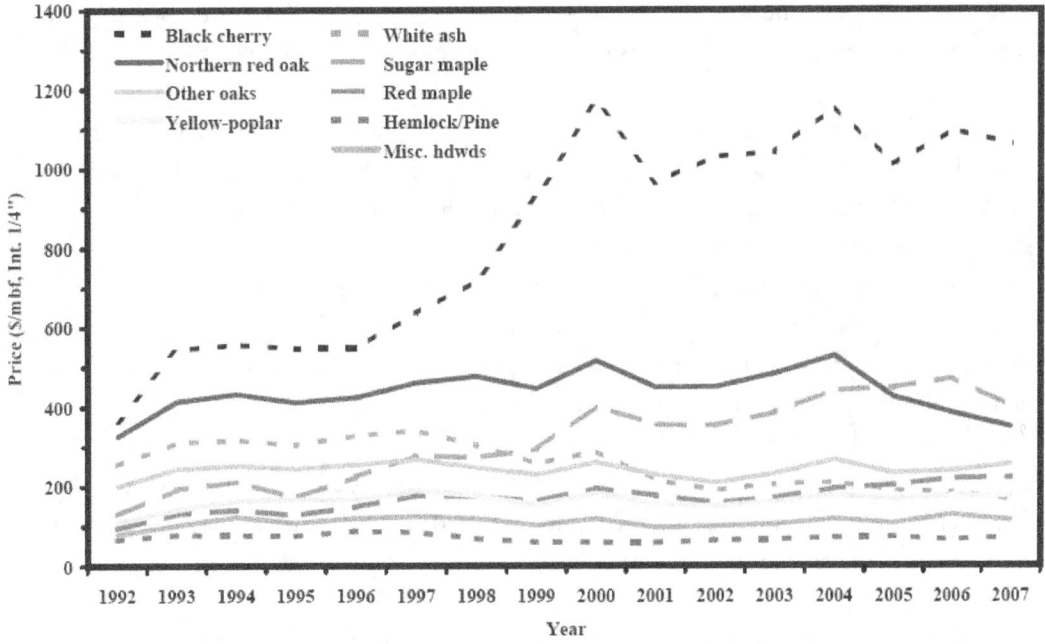

Figure 1.5.—Stumpage prices paid for the commercial tree species in Pennsylvania from 1992 to 2007. Other oaks include all oak species except northern red oak. Miscellaneous hardwoods include species such as aspen, American beech, black birch, yellow birch, and cucumbertree. (Adapted from Jacobsen and Finley 2007)

# The Oak Regeneration Problem

There are thousands of papers published on the problems associated with regenerating oaks. Briefly, the oak regeneration problem occurs when the probability of replacing an existing oak stand with a new one by a final timber harvest or other stand-replacing disturbance is zero or unacceptably low for the stated management objective. In other words, the timber harvest is poorly timed with the oak regeneration process. Even-aged oak forests pass through a regeneration process that often spans 20 or more years. First, acorns must be produced and a sufficient number must survive to germinate and establish new oak seedlings. These seedlings must survive long enough to develop root systems and stems that can compete successfully for dominant positions once a new forest is initiated by a timber harvest. If the harvest occurs before oak seedlings are established or they are able to build large root systems, then it is highly unlikely that a new oak forest will form. The purpose of SILVAH and this publication is to provide guidance to forest managers in the sequence and timing of silvicultural treatments designed to foster the development of small oak regeneration to competitively sized reproduction that can form new oak stands following a timber harvest.

# SILVAH

The SILVAH decision support system (Marquis and Ernst 1991, Marquis and others 1992) originally emerged from Allegheny Hardwood Silviculture Training Sessions offered by U.S. Forest Service and the Pennsylvania State University Cooperative Extension (PSU) beginning in 1978. These sessions were designed to help forest land managers integrate the latest findings from regeneration and other silvicultural research into practice. The approach taken in the early training sessions was to help land managers plan inventories that would enable them to recognize when individual stands met key thresholds that indicated readiness for specific silvicultural prescriptions. For example, the overstory inventory yielded data about average tree size and stocking that could be used to recognize the necessity for a thinning treatment, or that a stand had reached maturity and was ready to regenerate. An understory inventory suggested the steps that were required to ensure successful regeneration after a harvest sequence.

Initially, these thresholds were represented as a series of independent decisions, building on research that was being published by the originators of SILVAH. Roach (1977) published a stocking guide that also included guidelines for thinning prescriptions, similar to work that Roach and Gingrich (1968) had prepared for central hardwood stands earlier in Roach's career. Grisez and Peace (1973) published guidelines that allowed managers to recognize stands that were stocked sufficiently with advance regeneration to ensure a fully stocked new stand of desired species after harvest. Over time, the independent guidelines merged into an integrated and quantitative approach to prescription development through inventory and analysis (Marquis and others 1975; Marquis and Bjorkbom 1982). This approach was encapsulated in a set of computer programs known as SILVAH (**Silv**iculture of **A**llegheny **H**ardwoods). The SILVAH programs included tools for data summary and analysis, writing stand descriptions, recommendations for silvicultural prescriptions, and a stand-growth simulator.

The SILVAH approach and software became the standard for silvicultural decisionmaking in Allegheny and northern hardwood stands on all public and large parcels of private land in northern Pennsylvania and extending into adjacent states. This decision-support framework included limited guidelines for oak which were not well tested or widely adopted. Many practitioners continued to rely on pencil and paper calculations using guidelines from Roach and Gingrich (1968) and other publications on oak regeneration by Sander and Clark (1971) and Sander and others (1976).

In 1999, the Silvicultural Advisory Committee of the Pennsylvania Bureau of Forestry (BOF) asked the Forest Service to strengthen the SILVAH decision framework as it applied to sustaining mixed-oak forests (Stout and others 2007). The approach adopted was to rely on expert opinion and research conducted in other regions in the short-run to restructure the decision framework and identify research needs. A group of scientists and land managers from the Forest Service, BOF, PSU, and private industry was convened in January 2000 to work on task.

Initially, draft interim guidelines were developed and key knowledge gaps identified (Stout and others 2007). BOF foresters were trained in the guidelines in a series of 2-day training courses that spring. The guidelines were tested in the field during 2000 and 2001. A follow-up meeting between Forest Service scientists and BOF foresters in January 2002 led to several additions, deletions, and changes in the draft interim guidelines. Field testing from 2002 to the present has resulted in only minor revisions. An annual training course in oak silviculture conducted jointly by the Forest Service and BOF in Brookville, Pennsylvania began in September 2002.

This publication is a result of that initial meeting as well as the subsequent interaction between the Forest Service and BOF personnel. It is for land managers interested in sustaining mixed-oak forests for whatever reason. Currently, this publication is limited to the oak forests of the mid-Atlantic region. However, it could apply to oak forests outside this region if used cautiously. Also, this publication focuses on even-age management.

The SILVAH inventory process for assessing the overstory and understory of oak stands is described in Chapter 2. In Chapter 3, we explain how SILVAH calculates key summary variables from that inventory data. Chapter 4 contains the decision charts that SILVAH navigates using key summary variables to arrive at a recommended prescription. Silvicultural treatments dealing with stand renewal and how to apply them correctly are described in Chapter 5. Chapter 6 includes three additional decision charts for assessing the success of the regeneration prescriptions. Early stand-management techniques for ensuring that desirable individual stems capture the growing space are discussed in this chapter too. A sample SILVAH printout and tally sheets are included in the Appendix.

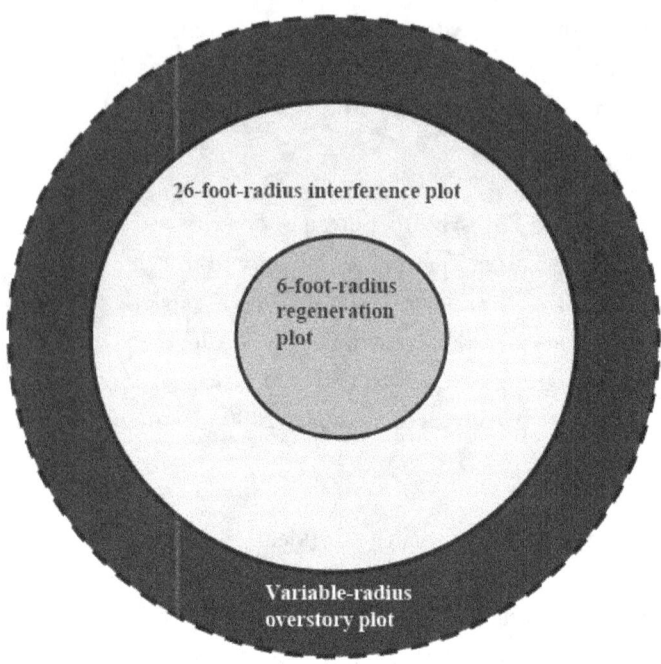

Figure 2.1.—The SILVAH inventory procedure uses nested plots to sample tree regeneration, interfering vegetation, deer browsing pressure, and overstory conditions.

# CHAPTER 2: INVENTORY PROCEDURES

Patrick Brose, Barbara McGuinness, and Susan Stout

One of the keys to accurately evaluating the regenerative potential of a mixed-oak stand is to simultaneously consider the species present, the abundance, size, and spatial distribution of reproduction and trees, and factors limiting successful regeneration. To accomplish this, SILVAH uses three nested plots that focus on tree regeneration, obstacles to successful regeneration, and overstory conditions (Fig. 2.1). In this chapter, we explain how to inventory mixed-oak stands using these three plots and record the data on the SILVAH tally sheets (Appendix 1 and 2).

## The Regeneration Plot

Reproduction can be tallied on a 3.7-foot or 6-foot radius plot (1/1000 or 1/385 acre). Generally, the 6-foot plot is used. For stands less than 10 acres, use two regeneration plots per acre. For stands of 10 acres or more, use 20 regeneration plots plus 2 additional plots for each 5 acres above 10 acres. For example, a 15-acre stand would have 22 regeneration plots and there would be 28 such plots in a 30-acre stand. Plots must be located systematically throughout the stand to ensure adequate spatial distribution.

A tally sheet is used to record regeneration data (Appendix 1). SILVAH simultaneously evaluates regeneration abundance and size by the "stocked plot" approach (Marquis and Bjorkbom 1982, Marquis and others 1975, Roach and Gingrich 1968). In this approach, stem counts for the different species groups are adjusted for size (taller stems are counted double) and are recorded as weighted counts.

## Oak Regeneration

The first reproduction to look for on the plot is oak regeneration. This is tallied into one of three categories based on height or root-collar diameter (RCD). **Competitive oak** are stems that are highly likely to be dominant or codominant at crown closure of the new stand following harvest of the overstory. These are stems more than 3 ft tall or with a RCD greater than 0.75 inches. All oak stump sprouts are tallied as competitive oak regardless of height. Record up to three stems per stump.

The RCD criterion is particulary important in assessing oak regeneration because root development rather than stem growth is emphasized when oaks are young (Brose 2007, Kolb and others 1990, Miller and others 2004a). In other words, an oak stem that is only a foot tall may have a large root system and is ready to compete in full sunlight (Fig. 2.2). Undersize oaks with a competitive root system usually can be identified as follows: they are 1 to 3 feet tall, have multiple stems originating from a common point, and have numerous (more than 20) full-size leaves (Brose 2007). They also tend to be white, black, chestnut, or scarlet oak and generally are found on intermediate and dry sites or in previously disturbed stands.

Site quality must be considered when evaluating competitive oak stocking because it will be increasingly likely that the reproduction of other hardwood species will outcompete oak regeneration as site quality improves. Account for site quality by weighting the count of competitive oak according to Table 2.1.

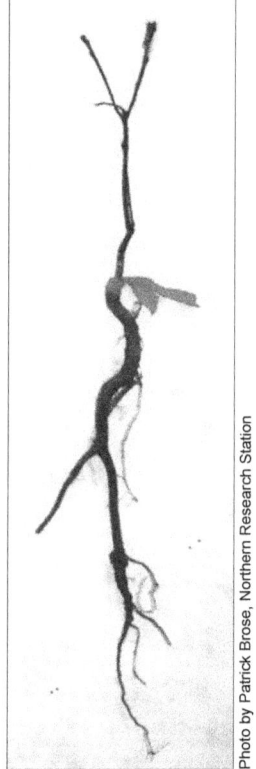

Figure 2.2.—A 4-year-old white oak seedling grown in full sunlight. The red line on the stem shows the location of the ground line before the seedling was excavated; the flagging marks the root collar. Note the characteristic emphasis of root development at the expense of stem growth.

Photo by Patrick Brose, Northern Research Station

### Table 2.1.—Weighting criteria for competitive oak regeneration

| | Oak site index or BOF site class | | |
| --- | --- | --- | --- |
| | High quality[b] | Medium quality | Low quality |
| Stem height or RCD[a] | >75 feet (1) | 55 to 75 feet (2) | <55 feet (3) |
| Height 3 to 7 feet<br>RCD 0.75 to 1.0 inch | 1 | 1 | 1 |
| Height 7 to 10 feet<br>RCD 1.0 to 1.5 inches | 2 | 3 | 5 |
| Height >10 feet<br>RCD >1.5 inches | 3 | 5 | 10 |

[a]RCD = root collar diameter.
[b]For example, a 4-foot-tall oak on any quality site is recorded as 1. An 8-foot-tall oak has a weighted count of 2 on a high-quality site, 3 on a medium-quality site, and 5 on a low-quality site. The weighted count for an 11-foot-tall oak is 3 on a high-quality site, 5 on a medium-quality site, and 10 on a low-quality site.

The next type of oak regeneration to look for is **established oak** reproduction. These are oak seedlings and sprouts that are too small to compete for a dominant or codominant canopy position after overstory removal on high-quality sites, but are large enough to take advantage of silvicultural treatments designed to help them develop to competitive size. Established oak is defined as stems 0.5 to 3.0 ft tall or with a RCD of 0.25 to 0.75 inch.

The last category of oak reproduction is **new oak** which are oak seedlings that are too small to be in the established oak category. If there is any question which category an oak stem should be assigned, record the stem in the smaller size class. For example, a borderline established/new oak would be tallied as a new oak.

### Other Regeneration

One of the goals of SILVAH is to promote diverse regeneration that will develop into mixed-species stands and not monocultures. To this end, SILVAH recognizes several other species and species groups that are acceptable associates in mixed-oak forests. Tallying criteria for these are from research (Marquis and Bjorkbom 1982, Marquis and others 1975) and expert opinion:

1) **Black cherry:** Count all seedlings at least 2 inches tall, with two normal-size leaves. Stems more than 1 foot tall are counted as two stems.

2) **Conifers:** Count any eastern hemlock (*Tsuga canadensis*), pine (*Pinus* spp.), or spruce (*Picea* spp.) seedling with two whorls or 0.5 to1.0 foot tall. Stems with three or more whorls or that are more than 1 foot tall are counted as two stems.

3) **Yellow-poplar:** Count all seedlings that are at least 2 inches tall with two normal-size leaves. Stems more than one foot tall are counted as two stems. Do not count yellow-poplar on sites where there are no dominant yellow-poplar trees in the canopy, generally upper slope and ridgetop, dry site positions, as this species is not a fast grower nor long lived on such sites.

4) **Other desirables:** These depend on the specific location and may or may not include species such as red maple, sugar maple, and cucumbertree (*Magnolia acuminata*). For example, red maple would be considered desirable regeneration in northwestern Pennsylvania but as interference in parts of the Ridge and Valley region. Count all seedlings that are at least 2 inches tall with two normal-size leaves. Stems more than 1 foot tall are counted as two stems. Maples must pass the tug test; that is they are not pulled out of the ground easily. Count all hickory (*Carya* spp.) and walnut (*Juglans* spp.) seedlings that meet established oak criteria. Those that meet competitive oak criteria are counted as two stems.

5) **Saplings:** If a past disturbance has allowed regeneration to grow into saplings (1 to 6-inch d.b.h.), tally them **if** they are a desirable species, have good form and vigor, and meet one of these density thresholds: two stems less than 2.0 inches d.b.h. or one stem 2 to 6 inches d.b.h. Record the code of the dominant species (Table 2.2). Note that sapling regeneration is an age class distinctly different from the overstory and undesirable or poorly-formed saplings are tallied as tall woody interference; see next section.

## Residuals

Pole-size (6 to 10 inch d.b.h) trees called residuals are sometimes retained after a final harvest to meet policy guidelines or for aesthetic, biodiversity, or wildlife values. Record residuals by the species code (Table 2.2) **if** they are a desirable species, have good form and vigor, and are rooted in the regeneration plot. Some examples of possible residuals in mixed-oak stands are butternut (*Juglans cinerea*), cucumbertree, eastern white pine (*P. strobus*), hickory, or Table Mountain pine (*P. pungens*). Note that residuals do not count toward the required regeneration stocking in oak stands and undesirable stems of this size class are tallied as tall woody interference, see next section).

## Tall Woody Interference

The final condition to record on the regeneration plot is the presence of tall woody interference. This category includes any woody species (undesirable sapling/pole or a poorly formed desirable stem) that will interfere with the regeneration of species desirable for the selected management objective. Tallying criteria are more than 6 feet tall and rooted in the regeneration plot. Undesirable woody stems rooted just outside the regeneration plot but overtop it also can be tallied as tall woody interference. Record the species code of the dominant tall woody interference on the plot (Tables 2.2-2.3). Note that what constitutes tall woody interference varies for numerous reasons. For example, American beech often is recorded as tall woody interference because it casts dense shade on the forest floor. However, it might be desirable where a strategy for identifying beech trees resistant to beech bark disease is in place. This is the only interference recorded from the regeneration plot; all other interference is evaluated on the 26-foot radius plot.

# The Interference Plot

Although the regeneration plot accounts for some of the positive attributes of the stand (the composition and stocking of the reproduction), the interference plot assesses competing vegetation, deer impact, and site limitations (Appendix 1). The interference plot has a 26-foot radius and there always is an interference plot with each regeneration plot.

## Competing Vegetation

**Low woody interference**. This group includes shrubs and small undesirable trees that are less than 6 feet tall and the foliage of taller trees that occur within this stratum. Visually estimate the proportion of the 26-foot plot shaded by all low woody interference. Record the estimation in 5-percent increments if it is less than 50 percent and in 10-percent increments if it is more than 50 percent. Record the species code for the dominant species (Tables 2.2-2.3).

**Fern**. Visually estimate the proportion of the 26-foot plot shaded ferns in 5-percent increments if cover is less than 50 percent and in 10-percent increments if cover is more than 50 percent. For species of fern that do not spread via rhizomes, e.g., wood fern (*Dryopteris intermedia*), adjust the estimated cover by dividing by two. For rhizomatous ferns such as hay-scented (*Dennstaedtia punctilobula*), New York (*Thelypteris noveboracensis*), or bracken (*Pteridium aquilinum*), do not adjust the estimated cover. Sum the two estimates to arrive at the percent cover for the entire plot. For example, a plot with 30 percent cover of hay-scented fern and 20 percent cover of wood fern would be recorded as 40 percent (30 percent + (20 percent ÷ 2)).

**Table 2.2.—Forest Service, mnemonic, and Pennsylvania Bureau of Forestry (BOF) codes for most common tree species of mid-Atlantic region (Marquis and others 1992)**

| Species | Forest Service | Mnemonic | BOF |
|---|---|---|---|
| Ash | 540 | A | 0 |
| Ash, black | 543 | BA | 0 |
| Ash, green | 544 | GA | 0 |
| Ash, white | 541 | WA | 55 |
| Aspen | 740 | ASP | 63 |
| Aspen, bigtooth | 743 | BTA | 0 |
| Aspen, quaking | 746 | QA | 0 |
| Balsam poplar | 741 | BP | 0 |
| Basswood, American | 951 | BAS | 58 |
| Beech, American | 531 | AB | 54 |
| Beech, blue | 391 | BB | 90 |
| Birch | 370 | B | 50 |
| Birch, gray | 379 | GRB | 0 |
| Birch, paper | 375 | PB | 0 |
| Birch, sweet | 372 | SB | 0 |
| Birch, yellow | 371 | YB | 0 |
| Blackgum | 693 | BG | 66 |
| Buckeye | 330 | BUC | 0 |
| Butternut | 601 | BUT | 71 |
| Catalpa | 542 | CAT | 0 |
| Cedar, northern white | 241 | NWC | 0 |
| Cherry, black | 762 | BC | 76 |
| Cherry, pin | 761 | PC | 95 |
| Chestnut, American | 421 | AMC | 0 |
| Chinkapin, Allegheny | 422 | ALC | 0 |
| Chokecherry | 763 | CC | 0 |
| Cottonwood, eastern | 742 | EC | 0 |
| Crabapple | 660 | CRB | 0 |
| Cucumbertree | 651 | CUC | 84 |
| Devil's Walking Stick | 353 | DWS | 89 |
| Dogwood | 491 | DOG | 81 |
| Elm | 970 | E | 61 |
| Elm, American | 972 | AE | 0 |
| Elm, rock | 977 | RE | 0 |
| Elm, slippery | 975 | SE | 0 |
| Fir, balsam | 012 | BF | 0 |
| Hackberry | 460 | HAC | 0 |
| Hawthorn | 500 | HAW | 94 |
| Hemlock, eastern | 261 | EH | 6 |
| Hickory | 400 | H | 60 |
| Hickory, bitternut | 402 | BH | 0 |
| Hickory, mockernut | 409 | MH | 0 |
| Hickory, shagbark | 407 | SGH | 0 |

**Continued**

**Table 2.2.—Continued.**

| Species | Forest Service | Mnemonic | BOF |
|---|---|---|---|
| Hickory, shellbark | 405 | SLH | 0 |
| Hickory, pignut | 403 | PH | 0 |
| Honeylocust | 552 | HL | 0 |
| Ironwood | 701 | OST | 92 |
| Larch | 070 | L | 0 |
| Locust, black | 901 | BL | 0 |
| Maple | 310 | M | 0 |
| Maple, boxelder | 313 | BEM | 0 |
| Maple, mountain | 319 | MTM | 0 |
| Maple, red | 316 | RM | 21 |
| Maple, silver | 317 | SVM | 0 |
| Maple, striped | 315 | STM | 99 |
| Maple, sugar | 318 | SM | 20 |
| Mountain ash | 935 | MTA | 97 |
| Oak | 800 | O | 0 |
| Oak, black | 837 | BO | 31 |
| Oak, blackjack | 824 | BJO | 0 |
| Oak, burr | 823 | BRO | 0 |
| Oak, chestnut | 832 | CO | 48 |
| Oak, chinkapin | 826 | CKO | 0 |
| Oak, northern pin | 809 | NPO | 0 |
| Oak, northern red | 833 | NRO | 30 |
| Oak, overcup | 822 | OO | 0 |
| Oak, pin | 830 | PNO | 0 |
| Oak, post | 835 | PO | 0 |
| Oak, scarlet | 806 | SO | 32 |
| Oak, shingle | 834 | SHO | 0 |
| Oak, southern red | 812 | SRO | 0 |
| Oak, swamp chestnut | 825 | SCO | 0 |
| Oak, swamp white | 804 | SWO | 0 |
| Oak, white | 802 | WO | 40 |
| Osage-orange | 641 | OSO | 0 |
| Paulownia | 712 | PAU | 0 |
| Pawpaw | 367 | PAW | 0 |
| Pecan | 404 | PCN | 0 |
| Persimmon | 521 | PER | 0 |
| Pine | 100 | P | 0 |
| Pine, Austrian | 136 | AUP | 2 |
| Pine, loblolly | 131 | LOB | 2 |
| Pine, pitch | 126 | PP | 0 |
| Pine, red | 125 | RP | 0 |
| Pine, Scotch | 130 | SCP | 2 |
| Pine, shortleaf | 110 | SLP | 2 |
| Pine, Table Mountain | 123 | TMP | 2 |

**Continued**

**Table 2.2.—Continued.**

| Species | Forest Service | Mnemonic | BOF |
|---|---|---|---|
| Pine, Virginia | 132 | VP | 0 |
| Pine, white | 129 | WP | 1 |
| Redcedar, eastern | 068 | ERC | 0 |
| Sassafras | 931 | SAS | 96 |
| Serviceberry | 355 | SVB | 91 |
| Sourwood | 711 | SW | 0 |
| Spruce | 090 | S | 0 |
| Spruce, black | 095 | BS | 0 |
| Spruce, Norway | 091 | NS | 0 |
| Spruce, red | 097 | RS | 0 |
| Spruce, white | 094 | WS | 0 |
| Sweetgum | 611 | SG | 0 |
| Sycamore, American | 731 | AS | 0 |
| Tamarack | 071 | TAM | 0 |
| Walnut, black | 602 | BW | 0 |
| Wild plum | 766 | PLM | 0 |
| Willow | 920 | W | 0 |
| Yellow-poplar | 621 | YP | 59 |
| Other hardwoods | 004 | OHW | 88 |
| Other softwoods | 001 | OSW | 0 |
| Other nonCommercial | 999 | ONC | 0 |

**Grass and Sedge.** Record the percentage of the interference plot that would be covered completely by all observed grass and sedge species as if they were all considered together. Record 1 percent even if only a trace of grass or sedge is present.

**Grapevine** (*Vitis* spp.). Record the number of grapevines rooted in the plot reaching into the forest canopy.

## Site Limitations

SILVAH recognizes three forest floor conditions that can impede stand renewal. If any is found anywhere on the 26-foot plot, record the corresponding number for the condition.

1) **Poor drainage.** The water table persists close to the soil surface during all or part of the growing season. In this environment, seedlings drown. Poor drainage is indicated by standing water, a black, greasy soil surface, or the presence of hydrophytic plants, e.g., jewelweed (*Impatiens pallida*), marsh marigold (*Calthra palustris*), and skunk cabbage (*Symplocarpus foetidus*).

2) **Rock/thin soil.** There is little soil overlaying large rocks or bedrock, making shallow-rooted regeneration vulnerable to desiccation in a dry growing season or in the harsh conditions following complete overstory removal. This is not the same as rocks overlaying deep soil like that found in the Ridge and Valley region.

**Table 2.3.—Forest Service, mnemonic, and Pennsylvania Bureau of Forestry codes (BOF) for most common shrub, trailing vine, and nonnative invasive species of mid-Atlantic region (Marquis and others 1992)**

| Shrub or vine species | Forest Service | Mnemonic | BOF |
|---|---|---|---|
| Blueberry | 786 | BLU | 0 |
| Blueberry, lowbush | 785 | LBL | 0 |
| Currant | 870 | CUR | 0 |
| Hazelnut | 501 | HAZ | 0 |
| Huckleberry | 549 | HUK | 0 |
| Mountain laurel | 733 | MTL | 0 |
| Prickly-ash | 638 | PRA | 0 |
| Rhododendron | 737 | RHO | 0 |
| Rubus | 915 | RUB | 0 |
| Witch-hazel | 585 | WHL | 0 |
| Winterberry | 593 | ILV | 0 |
| Other woody shrubs | 996 | OWS | 0 |
| Poison-ivy | 867 | PI | 0 |
| Virginia creeper | 715 | VCR | 0 |
| Nonnative invasive species | | | |
| Ailanthus | 998 | AIL | 98 |
| Barberry | 368 | BAR | 0 |
| Buckthorn | 895 | BTH | 0 |
| Buckthorn, common | 846 | COB | 0 |
| Buckthorn, glossy | 847 | GLB | 0 |
| Garlic Mustard | 382 | GLM | 0 |
| Honeysuckle, amur | 639 | AHN | 0 |
| Honeysuckle, bush | 635 | LON | 0 |
| Honeysuckle, Japanese | 636 | JHN | 0 |
| Honeysuckle, Tatarian | 637 | THN | 0 |
| Knotweed, Japanese | 385 | JAK | 0 |
| Maple, Norway | 320 | NWM | 0 |
| Multiflora rose | 905 | ROS | 0 |
| Olive, autumn | 535 | AUO | 0 |
| Olive, Russian | 534 | ELA | 0 |
| Oriental bittersweet | 384 | ORB | 0 |
| Stiltgrass, Japanese | 383 | JST | 0 |
| Other nonnative shrubs | 995 | NNS | 0 |

3) **Thick duff.** This condition sometimes occurs in conjunction with ericaceous shrubs, e.g., blueberry (*Vaccinium* spp.), huckleberry (*Gaylussacia* spp.), and mountain laurel (*Kalmia latifolia*) thickets, or conifer-dominated areas and can be a formidable obstacle for roots of new seedlings to penetrate. Thick duff is indicated by soil that feels spongy under foot.

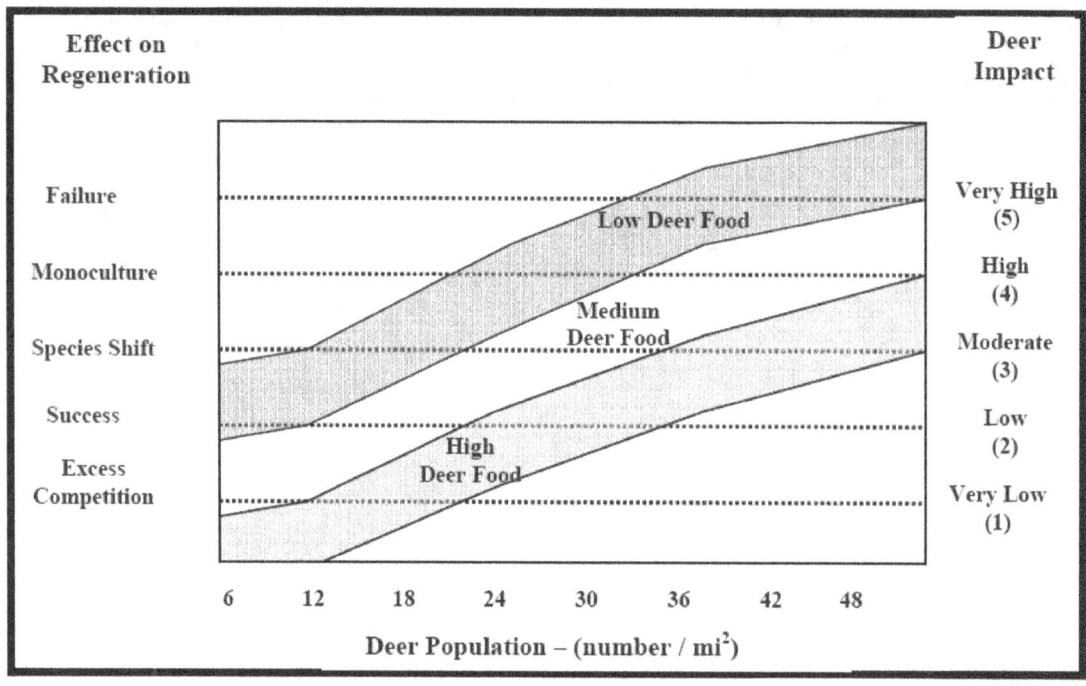

Figure 2.3.—Deer Impact Index for estimating the likely outcome of regeneration prescriptions given the deer density and availability of browse (redrawn from Marquis and others 1992). To use the chart, estimate the deer density and the amount of deer food and find the point where they intersect. From there, look to the right to determine the deer impact rating and to the left to determine the likely result of a timber harvest. For example, at a deer density of 30/mi² and low deer food (uncut, mature forest), the deer impact is very high and a timber harvest will likely result in a regeneration failure. At medium deer food (managed forest of several seral stages), deer impact drops to moderate and the outcome of a timber harvest is a species shift in the regeneration pool. At high deer food (managed forest interspersed with farmland), deer impact is low and a timber harvest will lead to successful forest regeneration.

### Deer Impact

This is an estimate of the amount of browsing pressure, which is a function of deer density and available food for deer (Fig. 2.3). SILVAH uses five levels of deer impact. Assess the estimated deer impact for several plots scattered throughout the stand using the following criteria and record the corresponding number (Fig. 2.4). At the end of the cruise, a single deer-impact level representing the average overall condition is assigned to the entire stand.

1) **Very low impact.** Found only inside well maintained, woven-wire, deer-exclosure fences.

2) **Low impact.** Desirable regeneration is abundant and of varying heights. Herbaceous plants such as Indian cucumberroot (*Medeola virginiana*), trillium (*Trillium* spp.), and wild lily-of-the-valley (*Maianthemum* spp.) are present and able to flower and fruit. Stump sprouts are present.

3) **Moderate impact.** Desirable regeneration is present but with little variability in height. Herbaceous plants are rare and there are no stump sprouts. Nonpreferred browse and browse-resistant plant species such as hay-scented fern, striped maple (*Acer pensylvanicum*), witch-hazel (*Hamamelis virginiana*), and beech root suckers are common and widespread.

4) **High impact.** Desirable regeneration is rare to absent. Nonpreferred and browse-resilient vegetation is limited in height growth by deer browsing.

Figure 2.4.—At Deer Impact Indices 1 and 2, forests have abundant oak regeneration that is able to respond to available light (upper two photos) and a diverse herbaceous plant community that is able to flower and fruit (middle two photos). At the Deer Impact Indices 3 and 4, stump sprouts are repeatedly browsed and nonpreferred plants become common and widespread (bottom two photos).

5) **Very high impact.** Desirable regeneration is absent. The abundance of nonpreferred vegetation is reduced by browsing. Browse-resilient plants show signs of heavy repeated browsing and a browse line is evident.

## Site Quality

The final information recorded on the interference plot is assignment of site quality. This evaluation is essential in oak stands for the SILVAH program to recommend a prescription. As with the deer-impact levels, site quality is assessed on several scattered plots and then a stand-level average is assigned at the end of the cruise. Rate the plot as high, medium, or low quality based on its location in the landscape, species composition, and height and number of logs of

**Table 2.4.—Characteristics of high-, medium-, and low-quality sites in mixed-oak forests of the mid-Atlantic region**

| Site quality | Characteristic |
| --- | --- |
| High | Moist, well drained, deep soils |
| | Protected coves, riparian areas, valley bottoms |
| | Northern red oak, white oak, yellow-poplar, hemlock |
| | Merchantable bole length >50 feet (> three 16-foot logs) |
| | Mature tree height >80 feet |
| Medium | Moderately drained, fairly deep soils that are intermittently dry |
| | Midslope topographic position |
| | Black oak, white oak, northern red oak, white pine |
| | Merchantable bole length 35-45 feet (2 - 2½ 16-foot logs) |
| | Mature tree height 65-80 feet |
| Low | Rocky, shallow soils that are chronically dry |
| | Ridges and upperslope topographic positions |
| | Chestnut oak, scarlet oak, pitch pine, mountain laurel |
| | Merchantable bole length <30 feet (< two 16-foot logs) |
| | Mature tree height <65 feet. |

the dominant tree species (Table 2.4). Care must be exercised if the dominant trees already have been removed from the stand or if the vegetation does not reflect the quality of the soil. In some cases, for example chestnut oak stands on medium-quality sites, determining site index might be required as site quality plays an important role in the oak decision charts. For example, a site index$_{50}$ 68 stand might receive a final harvest prescription whereas a site index$_{50}$ 72 stand would undergo a shelterwood sequence.

**Optional Understory Assessments**

SILVAH includes two options for enhancing understory assessment that might be helpful in some circumstances. One is recording the presence of nonnative invasive plant species (NNIS). To use this option, record the species code (Table 2.3) of any NNIS found in the plots or observed in or near the stand. SILVAH generates short ecological descriptions for 18 commonly found NNIS (3 tree, 12 shrub, 1 forb, 1 vine, 1 grass) in the mid-Atlantic region. No recommended treatments are given for controlling these species so the user must consult an extension service, other Forest Service information sources, or obtain that information via the Internet.

The second option is the third-decade oak stocking prediction from the "Oak Regeneration Guidelines for the Central Appalachians (Steiner and others 2008). This option may benefit foresters who are unsure whether they already have sufficient oak regeneration to meet their management objectives. This option consists of two approaches. When inventorying stands, determine the aggregate height of oak seedlings rooted within 3.7 feet of the center of each regeneration plot as per the instructions in the Central Appalachian Oak Regeneration Guidelines. If the aggregate height data is not collected or if inventory data already have been collected, SILVAH will estimate the aggregate height by converting the seedling counts in each plot by the following equation where X is the oak seedling count for each of the three size classes:

$$\text{Aggregate Height} = ((X_{new} \div 2.6) \times 0.25) + ((X_{estbl} \div 2.6) \times 0.50) + ((X_{comp} \div 2.6) \times 3.0)$$

For example, a 6-foot regeneration plot containing 31 new oak, 10 established oak, and 3 competitive oak would have an estimated aggregate height of 7 feet [((31 ÷ 2.6) x 0.25) + ((10 ÷ 2.6) x 0.50) + ((2 ÷ 2.6) x 3.0)] = (2.98) + (1.92) + (2.31) = 7.21. Note that this is an estimate and that the preferred method in using the Central Appalachian Oak Regeneration Guidelines is to collect the data in the field according to instructions. Note that the Central Appalachian Oak Regeneration Guidelines were developed from data collected in south-central Pennsylvania and have not been tested elsewhere in Pennsylvania or outside of the State.

## The Overstory Plot

Inventorying the overstory entails collecting basal-area data by species, diameter, and stem quality (Appendix 2). This should be done immediately **after** the understory plot is inventoried at the rate of one overstory plot for every two regeneration plots because the canopy is usually less variable than the overstory. However, overmature stands and those disturbed recently may require that the overstory be sampled more frequently to ensure accurate results.

The overstory can be inventoried using fixed-area or variable-radius sampling techniques. For purposes of illustration here, we describe overstory inventory techniques using variable-radius sampling with a 10-factor prism as this is the conventional practice. At a minimum, data must be collected on species, diameter, and stem quality. Depending on management objectives, the overstory inventory can be expanded to include data on number of logs, grade, defects, canopy health, and wildlife value.

### Required Data

Collect data on trees more than 1.0 inch d.b.h. that are "in" according to a 10-factor prism. Trees selected by the prism are identified as to species, measured for d.b.h., and evaluated for quality. On the tally sheet, species is recorded in one of three ways: the Forest Service species code, a mnemonic code, or a user-defined code (Table 2.2).

D.b.h. can be either estimated or measured and recorded by 1- or 2-inch size classes. For example, trees that are 15.50 to 16.49 inches d.b.h. are recorded as 16 inches when using the 1-inch class. With the 2-inch class, trees that are 15.00 to 16.99 inches d.b.h. are recorded as 16 inches. If estimated, d.b.h. should be recorded in 2-inch classes.

Quality is recorded as 1 for acceptable growing stock (AGS), 2 for unacceptable growing stock (UGS), or 3 for dead (Table 2.5). Acceptable growing stock is trees of a desirable species that contain at least one log, or will in the future, and likely will persist for another 15 years. Unacceptable growing stock is trees of an undesirable species, or do not contain at least one log and never will, or are unlikely to live another 15 years. If there is any question about the correct quality class for the tree, give it the benefit of the doubt, e.g., a questionable AGS/UGS is

**Table 2.5.—Codes and descriptions for determining tree quality and butt-log grade**

| Code | Description for tree quality | Code | Description for log grade |
|---|---|---|---|
| 1 | Acceptable Growing Stock (AGS) – Trees must meet all of the following criteria to be considered AGS.<br><br>a. Desirable species.<br>b. Contains a merchantable 8-foot bolt somewhere in their bole at this time or will contain an 8-foot bolt in the future.<br>c. Healthy enough to live another 15 years. | 1 | Factory-lumber log grade 1. |
| | | 2 | Factory-lumber log grade 2. |
| | | 3 | Factory-lumber log grade 3. |
| | | 4 | Locally defined log product (pallet log, local-use log). Construction log grade. |
| 2 | Unacceptable Growing Stock (UGS) – Trees meeting any of the following criteria are considered to be UGS.<br><br>a. Undesirable species.<br>b. Does not contain a merchantable 8-foot bolt anywhere in their bole at this time.<br>c. Never will contain a merchantable 8-foot bolt in the future.<br>d. Is unlikely to live another 15 years. | 5 | Locally defined bulk product such as boltwood. |
| | | 6 | Pulpwood – Contains at least two contiguous 4-foot bolts with a minimum top inside diameter of 4.0 inches and is at least 50 percent sound. |
| | | 7 | Fuelwood (same as pulpwood except minimum top inside diameter is 1.0 inch). |
| | If there is doubt whether a tree is AGS or UGS, consider it AGS. Quality determination is not a cut-leave tally. | 8 | Cull – Tree is less than 50-percent sound or does not qualify for any of the grades or products listed. |
| 3 | Dead – Standing dead trees. | 9 | Veneer log. |

recorded as AGS. Quality determination is not a cut-leave tally as a partial cut likely will remove most or all of the low-quality trees classified as AGS.

When the prism detects a borderline tree (one that cannot be positively identified as in or out), the most accurate procedure is to measure the horizontal distance in feet from the plot center to the center of the tree at d.b.h. If that distance is more than 2.75 times d.b.h., then the tree is out; otherwise it is in. A quicker method is to tally it as half a tree by recording its species and d.b.h. and then adding 5 to its quality designation, i.e., AGS is 6, UGS is 7, and dead is 8. Do not record every other borderline tree. This approach can lead to large errors in the estimated basal area.

**Optional Data**

If desired or needed to meet management objectives, additional data can be collected from the overstory plot to provide more complete information. Optional data include number of sawlogs, log grade, log defect, crown health, and certain wildlife-habitat attributes (Table 2.5 and 2.6). Note that these data will not influence the final silvicultural recommendation.

SILVAH uses equations from northwestern Pennsylvania to estimate number of sawlogs from d.b.h. (Fig. 2.5). If more accurate volumes are needed, the number of 8-foot bolts can be recorded for each tree containing a saw log. Estimates of the number of bolts should be from probable stump height to the point where diameter drops below the minimal merchantability size for the specific area or at the height that the bole breaks up.

The bottom-most two bolts (16 feet) can also be evaluated for grade and defect on scales of 1 to 9 to further refine the volume estimation. Grading criteria follow Rast and others (1973)

**Table 2.6.—Codes and descriptions for evaluating crown health and wildlife value of trees**

| Code | Description |
|------|-------------|
| | Crown Health |
| 1 | Healthy – Tree has less than 10-percent crown dieback or other abnormalities. |
| 2 | Good – Dieback of 10 to 25 percent or other abnormalities. |
| 3 | Fair – Dieback of 25 to 50 percent or other abnormalities. |
| 4 | Poor – Tree has more than 50-percent dieback, branch mortality, or other abnormalities. |
| | Wildlife Trees |
| 1 | Potential den tree – Live tree with large dead branch or broken top that may develop into a cavity in the future. |
| 2 | Existing den tree – Live tree with natural or artificial cavity (excludes small feeding holes made by pileated woodpeckers). |
| 3 | Snag with potential den – Dead or nearly dead tree at least 4 inches in d.b.h. and at least 10 feet tall, but no visible cavities. |
| 4 | Snag with existing den – Dead or nearly dead tree of the same minimum size as No. 3 above, but contains an existing den cavity. |

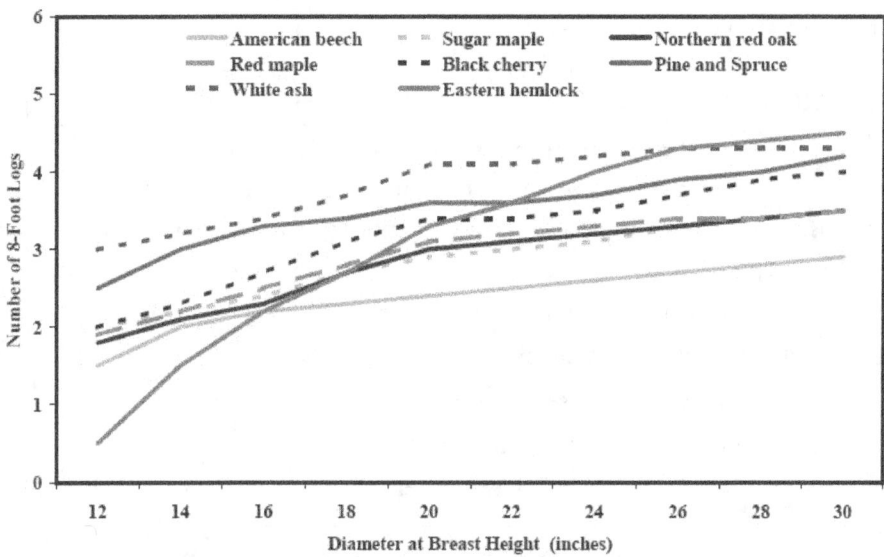

Figure 2.5.—Average number of 8-foot logs found in major commercial tree species of northwestern Pennsylvania (redrawn from Marquis and others 1992).

and Hanks and others (1980) and are explained in detail in Table 2.5. The user grades all trees, grades none, or only grades sawtimber-size trees that contain only pulpwood or are cull trees. If the second or third options are used, SILVAH applies log grades based on volume equations from Wiant and Yandle (1984) and Wiant (1986). Defect is estimated to the nearest 10 percent and recorded as a single digit (50-percent defect is recorded as a 5).

Crown condition can be rated for each tree using the North American Maple Project health guidelines of Millers and others (1991). These rating guidelines categorize crown condition in four classes: healthy, good, fair, and poor (Table 2.6).

**Table 2.7.—Restrictions of the silvicultural systems in SILVAH**

| Restriction | Description |
|---|---|
| No restrictions | None of the silvicultural systems (clearcut, shelterwood, group selection, or single tree selection) are excluded. The site can be regenerated without retaining trees from the previous stand. |
| No clearcutting | Some trees from the previous stand must be retained until the end of the regeneration process. Shelterwood, group selection, and single-tree selection are acceptable; clearcut is excluded. |
| No even-age | An intermittent high canopy must be maintained. Trees can be harvested only in small areas that range in size from single- to multiple-tree gaps. Group and single-tree selection are acceptable; clearcut and shelterwood are excluded. |
| No multiple-tree gaps | A continuous high canopy must be maintained. Trees can be harvested only in single-tree gaps. Only single-tree selection is acceptable; clearcut, shelterwood, and group selection are excluded. |

The important wildlife habitat of den trees also can be recorded as part of an overstory inventory. These can be designated as live trees or snags with existing cavities or the potential development of a cavity (Table 2.6).

## Stand-Level Information

The final two steps in a SILVAH cruise are for the user to make decisions about how the stand will be managed and record basic stand-level information on the understory tally sheet (Appendix 1). The user-provided decisions address five questions that must be answered to run the SILVAH decision-support system.

1) What are the restrictions on the silvicultural system?

2) Which set of prescription charts is desired?

3) Do you intend to start a regeneration sequence at this time?

4) Do you want to increase stocking of competitive oak?

5) Do you want to retain residual trees post-harvest?

The restrictions question determines which of the four silvicultural systems (clearcut, shelterwood, group selection, and single-tree selection) is acceptable (Table 2.7). The four restrictions are arranged in order of increasing exclusivity. The first two restrictions, "No restriction" and "No clearcutting" usually lead to even-age prescriptions and are the preferred choices for regenerating oak forests. The final two restrictions, "No even-aged" and "No multiple-tree canopy gaps" result in uneven-age prescriptions. Note that, at this time, choosing either of the uneven-age restrictions will result in SILVAH producing a prescription without special measures to promote oak and; on high-quality sites, such prescriptions will eventually result in conversion to another forest type.

The "prescription chart" question determines whether SILVAH should use the Allegheny/ northern hardwood or the mixed oak charts to arrive at a recommended treatment for the stand. The Allegheny and northern hardwood charts give no special consideration to the proportion of oak in the regeneration; they are simply among the desirable species considered in assessing regeneration stocking. The mixed-oak charts focus on cultivating a strong oak component in the regeneration and reflect the complex timing and sequences of treatments that mimic the historical disturbance regime that perpetuated oak forests.

The "start regenerating now" question gives the user the option to bypass SILVAH's default stand maturity criterion (18-inch mean diameter of merchantable-size stems (MDM) or less than 35 percent AGS trees in the overstory). This is important when the forest manager wishes to begin a regeneration sequence for a reason other than stand maturity. For example, a forest manager might want to regenerate a 15-inch MDM oak stand on a poor-quality site because it is unlikely that the 18-inch MDM threshold will ever be reached. Other examples of where regenerating sub 18-inch MDM oak stands might be desirable are in anticipation of imminent insect defoliation or landscape management plan considerations. To access the SILVAH regeneration prescriptions in these cases, the forest manager must choose "Yes" as the answer to this question.

The "increase oak" question refers to whether the proportion of competitive oak in the regeneration should be favored at the expense of other desirable reproduction during the silvicultural treatments. Forest managers who wish to emphasize oak in the new stand should answer "Yes" to this question. The third-decade stocking model described by Steiner and others (2008) may be helpful in answering this question if the stand meets the site quality and physiographic limitations of that model.

The question about postharvest residuals addresses the practice of retaining some trees to meet policy guidelines or objectives related to aesthetics, diversity, or wildlife values. Manager wishing to retain some trees from the current stand into the new one for any reason must answer "Yes" to this question.

Identification information is retained for record-keeping purposes. Some data can be recorded before the cruise; the remainder are recorded later. Precruise information includes the name of the landowner (U.S. Forest Service, Pennsylvania Bureau of Forestry, John Doe, etc.), name of the forest (Allegheny National Forest, Elk State Forest, North Woodlot, etc.), county of the stand, its acreage, and year of origin if known.

Finally, deer impact and site-index/site-quality information from the understory inventory are recorded as both indexes are important in SILVAH's decisionmaking process.

# CHAPTER 3: KEY DECISION VARIABLES

**Patrick Brose, Peter Knopp, and Susan Stout**

To arrive at an appropriate prescription for a stand, data collected on factors such as desirable seedling regeneration, interfering plants, site quality, deer impact, and overstory shading are summarized into a set of key decision variables and reported in various sections of a SILVAH printout (Appendix 3). These variables are evaluated against thresholds established from research and forestry practice according to the "stocked plot" concept (Marquis and Bjorkbom 1982, Marquis and others 1975, Roach and Gingrich 1968). The "stocked plot" concept is that for any key decision variable, a minimum, per-plot, threshold has been established and any plot exceeding that minimum threshold is considered stocked. For example, the minimum threshold for a plot to be stocked with fern interference is 30-percent coverage. A plot with 20-percent fern coverage is not considered stocked while a plot with 35-percent fern coverage is considered stocked.

## Understory

### Regeneration Stocking

SILVAH determines regeneration stocking for the species and species groups recorded in the field. The number of qualifying stems recorded on the data collection sheet for each plot is compared to the minimum number of stems in Table 3.1. This minimum threshold is closely tied to deer impact and varies by species and species group. For example, a plot containing 60 new oak would be stocked at deer impact levels 1 to 3 inclusive, but not at deer impact

**Table 3.1.—Stocking criteria (weighted stems/plot) for species and species groups**

| Species or group | Deer Impact Index | | | | |
|---|---|---|---|---|---|
| | 1 | 2 | 3 | 4 | 5 |
| Black cherry | 10 | 15 | 20 | 25 | 50 |
| Conifers | 2 | 5 | 15 | 25 | 50 |
| Competitive oak (Low[a]) | 1 | 1 | 1 | 1 | 1 |
| Competitive oak (Med[a]) | 2 | 2 | 2 | 2 | 2 |
| Competitive oak (High[a]) | 3 | 3 | 3 | 3 | 3 |
| Established oak | 12 | 12 | 25 | 50 | 100 |
| New oak | 25 | 25 | 50 | 100 | 200 |
| Other desirables | 15 | 30 | 50 | 100 | 200 |
| Yellow-poplar | 1 | 5 | 10 | 50 | 100 |
| Saplings (<2 inches d.b.h.) | 2 | 2 | 2 | 2 | 2 |
| Saplings (2-6 inches d.b.h.) | 1 | 1 | 1 | 1 | 1 |
| Residuals | (not counted toward regeneration stocking in oak stands) | | | | |
| Competitive desirables | 15 | 30 | 50 | 100 | 200 |
| Established desirables | 15 | 30 | 50 | 100 | 200 |
| Total oak | 25 | 25 | 50 | 100 | 200 |

[a]Refers to site quality.

24

**Table 3.2.—Expected percentage of oak stumps that will sprout after cutting**

| Species | D.b.h of parent tree (inches) | | | |
|---|---|---|---|---|
| | 2 to 5 | 6 to 11 | 12 to 16 | 17+ |
| Black oak | 85 | 65 | 20 | 5 |
| Chestnut oak | 100 | 90 | 75 | 50 |
| Northern red oak | 100 | 60 | 45 | 30 |
| Scarlet oak | 100 | 85 | 50 | 20 |
| White oak | 80 | 50 | 15 | 0 |

levels 4 or 5. In the case of competitive oak, site quality also is considered. For instance, a plot containing two competitive oaks would be stocked on low- and medium-quality sites but not on a high-quality site.

SILVAH also sums the counts of the different species and species groups to make three calculated regeneration variables: Competitive Desirables, Established Desirables, and Total Oak. Competitive Desirables is the sum of the non-oak counts plus the count of Competitive Oak. Established Desirables is the sum of Competitive Desirables plus the count of Established Oak. Total Oak is the sum of the count of Competitive Oak plus the counts of Established Oak and New Oak. These variables are important where the mix of regeneration fails to meet any stocking criterion, but the sum meets an appropriate threshold.

**Oak Stump Sprout Stocking**

An important source of oak regeneration is sprouting of the overstory oaks after they are harvested (Sander and others 1984). Sprouting probability of mature oaks varies considerably among the species and decreases as size class increases (Sander and others 1984). SILVAH calculates an estimated contribution of oak stump sprouts to regeneration stocking for a given stand based on the basal area of various oak species in the overstory. Table 3.2 shows the percentage of stems per acre expected to sprout for each square foot of oak basal area in the overstory by species and size class (Sander and others 1984).

SILVAH estimates the number of trees per acre in each of these size classes and converts these estimated numbers of sprouting stumps per acre to stocking percentages using the values in Table 3.3. SILVAH imposes an upper limit on the allowable contribution of stump sprouts to regeneration stocking. On poor-quality sites, the limit on the allowable contribution to regeneration stocking from stump sprouts is 60 percent. On medium- and good-quality sites, the limits are 40 and 20 percent, respectively. Conversely, SILVAH discounts the contribution of stump sprouts as the Deer Impact Index rises because deer preferentially browse stump sprouts. For example, at deer impact 3, approximately twice the number of sprouting stumps is needed to produce the same stocking levels as deer impact 1 or 2. At deer impact 4 and 5, stump sprouts do not add anything to regeneration stocking.

**Summary Variables**

The decision charts use a number of summary variables. For example, a summary variable called Any Competitive Regeneration is used frequently to help determine whether a stand is ready

**Table 3.3.—Factors for converting expected oak sprouts to a stocking equivalent**

| Site and Deer Impact Index | Sprouting stumps per acre (percent stocking equivalent)[a] | | | |
|---|---|---|---|---|
| High, 1 and 2 | 21-45 (5) | 46-71 (10) | 72-96 (15) | 97+ (20) |
| Med., 1 and 2 | 21-45 (10) | 46-71 (20) | 72-96 (30) | 97+ (40) |
| Low, 1 and 2 | 21-45 (15) | 46-71 (30) | 72-96 (45) | 97+ (60) |
| High, 3 | 46-96 (5) | 97-146 (10) | 147-197 (15) | 198+ (20) |
| Med., 3 | 21-45 (10) | 46-71 (20) | 72-96 (30) | 97+ (40) |
| Low, 3 | 21-45 (15) | 46-71 (30) | 72-96 (45) | 97+ (60) |
| High, 4 and 5 | At these deer impact levels, stump | | | |
| Med., 4 and 5 | sprouts will not contribute to regeneration | | | |
| Low, 4 and 5 | success regardless of site quality. | | | |

[a]For example, a stand with 100 sprouting stumps on a high-quality site with a Deer Impact Index of 2 adds 20 percent to the regeneration stocking total. At deer impact index 3, stocking drops to 10 percent. At deer levels 4 and 5, stocking is zero.

for a final removal cut. These are logical variables that summarize the information included in the individual species and species groups. All of these are calculated internally by SILVAH. The list that follows defines these variables. Note that SILVAH provides these summary regeneration stocking values at the ambient deer impact and as if a woven-wire fence is erected and maintained (Deer Impact Index 1).

1) **Any Competitive Regeneration:** A plot is stocked with Any Competitive Regeneration if it meets the stocking criteria for any of the regeneration categories in Table 3.1 except New Oak, Established Oak, Established Desirables, and Total Oak. The value reported on the SILVAH printout is the percentage of plots that meet any of these criterion plus the Stump Sprout Contribution to Regeneration Stocking calculated from the overstory inventory and Table 3.3.

2) **Any Competitive Regeneration or Residuals:** Same as No. 1 except any plot containing a residual tree also is included.

3) **Any Established Regeneration:** A plot is stocked with Any Established Regeneration if it meets the stocking criteria for any of the regeneration categories in Table 3.1 except New Oak and Total Oak. The value reported on the SILVAH printout is the percentage of plots that meet any criterion plus the Stump Sprout Contribution to Regeneration Stocking calculated from the overstory inventory and Table 3.3.

4) **All Established Oak:** A plot is stocked with All Established Oak if it meets the stocking criteria for Established Oak or Competitive Oak in Table 3.1. The value reported on the SILVAH printout is the percentage of plots that meet any criterion plus the Stump Sprout Contribution to Regeneration Stocking calculated from the overstory inventory and Table 3.3.

5) **All Oak:** A plot is stocked with All Oak if it meets the stocking criteria for New Oak, Established Oak, Competitive Oak, or Total Oak. The value reported on the SILVAH printout is the percentage of plots that meet any criterion plus the Stump Sprout Contribution to Regeneration Stocking calculated from the overstory inventory and Table 3.3.

**Table 3.4.—Thresholds for considering a plot stocked with various types of interference**

| Type of interference | Critical value | Plot size evaluated |
|---|---|---|
| Tall woody | 1 stem | 6-foot radius |
| Low woody | 30 percent | 26-foot radius |
| Fern | 30 percent | 26-foot radius |
| Grass | 30 percent | 26-foot radius |
| Grapevine | 1 vine | 26-foot radius |

### Stocking of Regeneration Obstacles

SILVAH calculates the percentage of plots that are stocked with various kinds of interfering plants and site limitations in the same manner as it determines regeneration stocking, except that these decision variables are independent of deer impact. Table 3.4 shows the stocking thresholds for each of the interfering plant variables. All plots on which site limitations were tallied are considered stocked with that limitation. SILVAH also calculates another summary variable: **Any Interference**. A plot stocked with any of the interfering vegetation types is considered to be stocked with Any Interference.

## Overstory

Just as SILVAH calculates key decision and summary variables from the understory data to help navigate the silvicultural charts and arrive at a recommended prescription, it does likewise with the overstory data. Important overstory information is provided on basal area by species and size class, volume and value estimations, stand diameters, relative density, effective age, and years to maturity.

SILVAH calculates basal areas using standard forest mensuration equations and does so for any tree species. An important basal area in SILVAH is that of undesirable saplings and poles. Ten square feet of basal area per acre of undesirable sapling/pole trees marks a shade threshold that must be addressed during a stand regeneration sequence (Miller and others 2004a). When this threshold is exceeded in a stand, SILVAH reports 70-percent stocking of tall woody interference and recommends some type of treatment. Volume estimates are from the Mesavage and Girard's (1946) volume tables and are based on the Doyle, International ¼-inch (default), or Scribner log rules. SILVAH applies log grades according to the hardwood volume equations of Wiant and Yandle (1984) and Wiant (1986) unless stand-specific data on log grade and defect are provided by the user.

Measures of stand diameter are: 1) the medial diameter of all trees more than 1.0-inch d.b.h. and 2) the mean diameter of the merchantable trees (MDM). This measure excludes trees less than 6.0 inches d.b.h. SILVAH considers a stand to be financially mature when the MDM reaches 18 inches (Marquis and others 1992).

SILVAH calculates three overstory decision variables (years to maturity, effective age, and relative density) that are important in navigating the decision charts. These are sometimes confusing to foresters so they are explained here in greater detail.

### Years to Maturity and Effective Age

Years to Maturity estimates how long it will be until the stand reaches 18 inches MDM. It is calculated from MDM, the financial maturity threshold, and one of two d.b.h. growth rates (0.15 inch/year for American beech, sugar maple, and all oaks (except northern red) or 0.20 inch/year for all other hardwoods) by the following equation:

$$\text{Years to Maturity} = (18' - \text{MDM}) / \text{Growth Rate}.$$

Initially, a projected maturity is calculated for each species in the overstory. These species-specific values are averaged and weighted by basal area to produce a standwide Years to Maturity. For example, a two-species stand with 50 percent of its basal area in northern red oak with an MDM of 16 inches and the remaining half in white oak with an MDM of 8 inches would have species-specific Years to Maturity of 10 and 67 years. The overall stand would have a Years to Maturity of 38 years.

Closely associated with Years to Maturity is Effective Age. Rather than the actual age of the stand as determined by increment coring, Effective Age is derived for individual species in the overstory and for the stand as a whole by the following equation:

$$\text{Effective Age} = [(\text{MDM} / \text{Growth Rate}) - \text{Years to Maturity}].$$

For instance, the northern red oak and white oak in the previous example would have individual effective ages of 80 and 53 years, respectively. The Effective Age for the stand would be 67 years.

### Relative Density

The major regeneration obstacle in mixed-oak forests throughout the Eastern United States is the dense shade cast by the overstory and midstory trees (Lorimer 1993, Lorimer and others 1994, Fig. 3.1). Quantifying this shade is important in prescribing an appropriate treatment but direct measures of shading are impractical during stand cruises. SILVAH uses relative density to fill this need as it is readily calculated from basal-area measurements that are routinely collected during stand examinations (Stout and Nyland 1986, Stout and others 1987).

Relative density is a measure of crowding or stocking among the trees of a stand and thus is correlated to the degree of understory shading. It is expressed as a proportion with a relative density of 100 percent, indicating a fully stocked stand, and is analogous of the A line on oak stocking charts (Gingrich 1967, McGill and others 1999). In addition to the basal area measurements, relative density also takes into account species, stand stratification, and crown shape. As a result, relative density provides a more realistic estimation of overstory crowding and subsequent shading of the forest floor than basal area.

Photo by Patrick Brose, Northern Research Station

Figure 3.1.—Dense understory shade inhibits the development of oak reproduction and is a major factor inhibiting oak regeneration throughout the eastern United States.

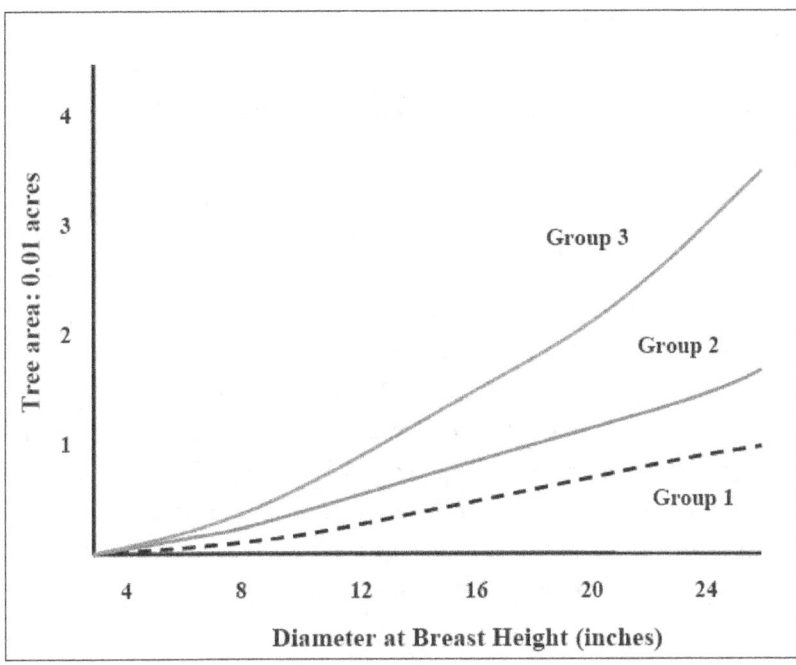

Figure 3.2.—Tree area curves for determining relative density. Group 1 includes black cherry, white ash, and yellow-poplar. Group 2 trees are northern red oak, red maple, and all species not specifically included in another group. Group 3 contains American beech, sugar maple, and all oaks except northern red oak. (Redrawn from Marquis and others 1992, Stout and others 1987).

SILVAH groups trees into three classes based on similarity of shade tolerance and growth rate for determining relative density (Stout and others 1987; Fig. 3.2). Group 1 contains trees that are fast-growing shade intolerants such as black cherry, white ash, and yellow-poplar. Group 2 species are intermediate in growth rate and shade tolerance. Northern red oak and red maple are representatives of Group 2 trees. Group 3 trees are shade tolerant and/or slow-growing species such as American beech, sugar maple, and white oak. Specific relative density equations for these three groups are:

G1: $RD = (183.35/d.b.h.^2) \times (0.0033033 + (0.020426 \times d.b.h.) + (0.0006776 \times d.b.h.^2)) \times BA$

G2: $RD = (183.35/d.b.h.^2) \times (-0.027142 + (0.024257 \times d.b.h.) + (0.0015225 \times d.b.h.^2)) \times BA$

G3: $RD = (183.35/d.b.h.^2) \times (-0.0027935 + (0.0058959 \times d.b.h.) + (0.004729 \times d.b.h.^2)) \times BA$

RD is relative density in percent, BA is basal area in square feet per tree, and d.b.h. is diameter at breast height in inches.

What this means is that the amount of shade cast on the forest floor by the overstory canopy is a function of species composition, bole diameter, and crown shape. For example, three hypothetical hardwood stands (A, B, C) have the same mean stem diameter (22 inches), same basal area ($\sim$106 ft$^2$), and all contain 40 trees per acre. They differ in species compositions; Stand A is pure black cherry, Stand B is pure northern red oak, and Stand C is pure white oak. Only Stand C is fully stocked; relative density is about 100 percent and shade is limiting development of the regeneration. The black cherry and red oak stands have abundant understory light for regeneration development, their relative densities are 31 and 51 percent, respectively.

# CHAPTER 4: THE DECISION CHARTS

**Patrick Brose, Kurt Gottschalk, Peter Knopp, Gary Miller, and Susan Stout**

At the heart of the SILVAH decision-support system are 11 dichotomous decision charts (A - K) that are navigated with the summary inventory data to a recommended prescription. The first five charts are revised versions of the Allegheny and northern hardwood decision charts published by Marquis and others (1992). Chart A is a steering chart; it helps determine which forest type (Allegheny/northern hardwood or mixed oak) is appropriate given user-defined management objectives and some site characteristics. Chart B provides uneven-age management prescriptions for stands containing sufficient stocking of desirable shade-tolerant species. It also contains a legend explaining the four prescription groups and their shading. The darker the shading, the more problematic the prescription will be to implement. Chart C is for thinning immature stands and is appropriate for either forest type. Charts D and E contain regeneration prescriptions for renewing Allegheny and northern hardwood stands.

There are six oak charts (F - K). Chart F contains prescriptions for releasing competitive oak reproduction on good-quality sites (oak $SI_{50}$ >70 feet). Chart G also is for high-quality sites but addresses how to enhance existing established oak seedlings so they can successfully compete after a future final harvest. Chart H is nearly identical to Chart F except it is for low- and medium-quality sites. In this chart, SILVAH treats established oak seedlings as if they were competitive sized, i.e., recommends final harvests in lieu of a shelterwood sequence. Chart I prescriptions promote development of new oak seedlings into the larger established oak size class. Charts J and K provide prescriptions aimed at establishing new oak seedlings via natural and artificial means, respectively.

Note that the oak charts are arranged in order of increasing regeneration difficulty. For example, the prescriptions on Chart F are easy and inexpensive to apply relative to those on Chart K.

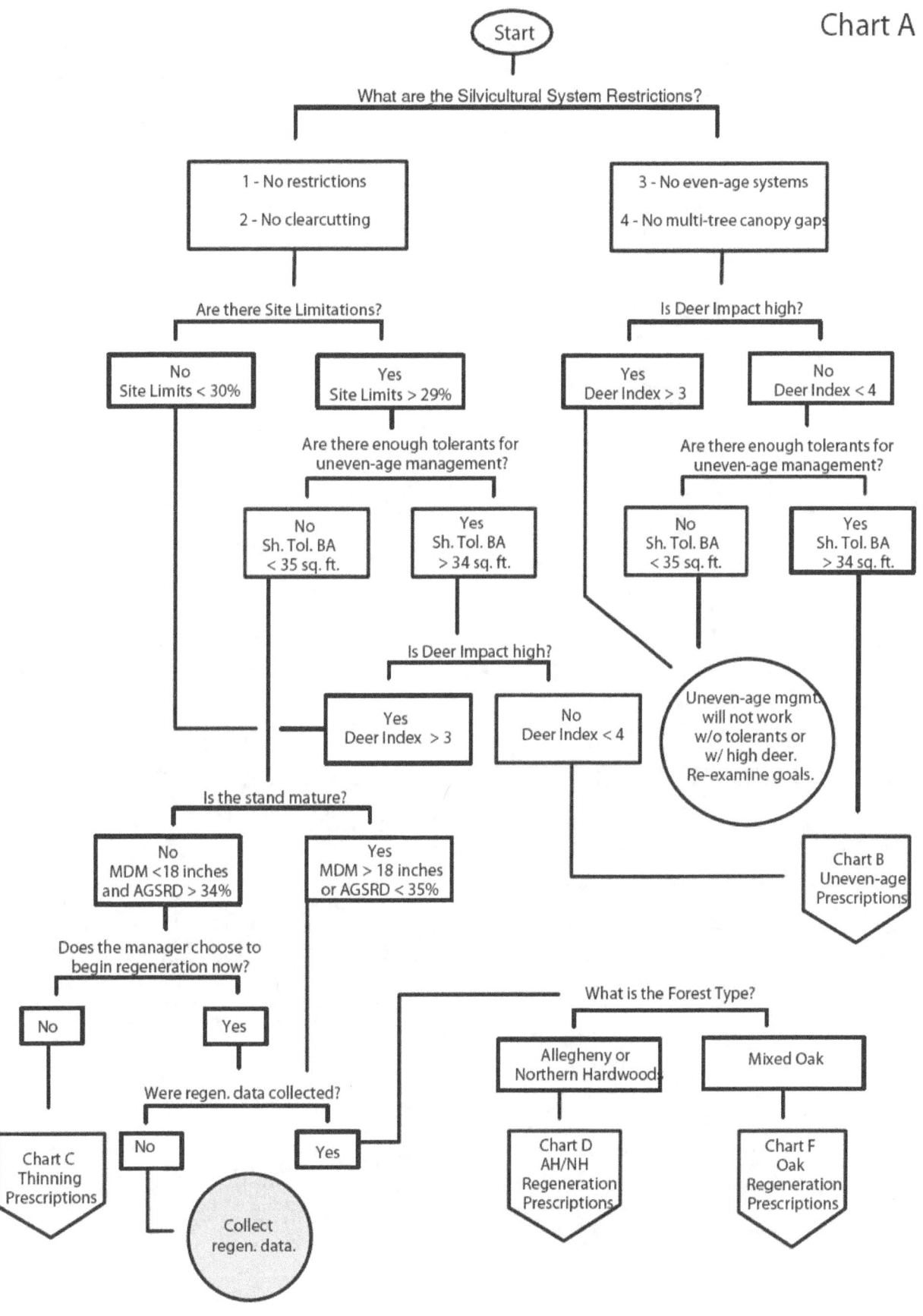

Start

What are the Silvicultural System Restrictions?

1 - No restrictions

2 - No clearcutting

3 - No even-age systems

4 - No multi-tree canopy gaps

Are there Site Limitations?

No
Site Limits < 30%

Yes
Site Limits > 29%

Is Deer Impact high?

Yes
Deer Index > 3

No
Deer Index < 4

Are there enough tolerants for
uneven-age management?

No
Sh. Tol. BA
< 35 sq. ft.

Yes
Sh. Tol. BA
> 34 sq. ft.

Are there enough tolerants for
uneven-age management?

No
Sh. Tol. BA
< 35 sq. ft.

Yes
Sh. Tol. BA
> 34 sq. ft.

Is Deer Impact high?

Yes
Deer Index > 3

No
Deer Index < 4

Uneven-age mgmt.
will not work
w/o tolerants or
w/ high deer.
Re-examine goals.

Chart B
Uneven-age
Prescriptions

Is the stand mature?

No
MDM <18 inches
and AGSRD > 34%

Yes
MDM > 18 inches
or AGSRD < 35%

Does the manager choose to
begin regeneration now?

No

Yes

What is the Forest Type?

Allegheny or
Northern Hardwoods

Mixed Oak

Were regen. data collected?

No

Yes

Chart C
Thinning
Prescriptions

Collect
regen. data.

Chart D
AH/NH
Regeneration
Prescriptions

Chart F
Oak
Regeneration
Prescriptions

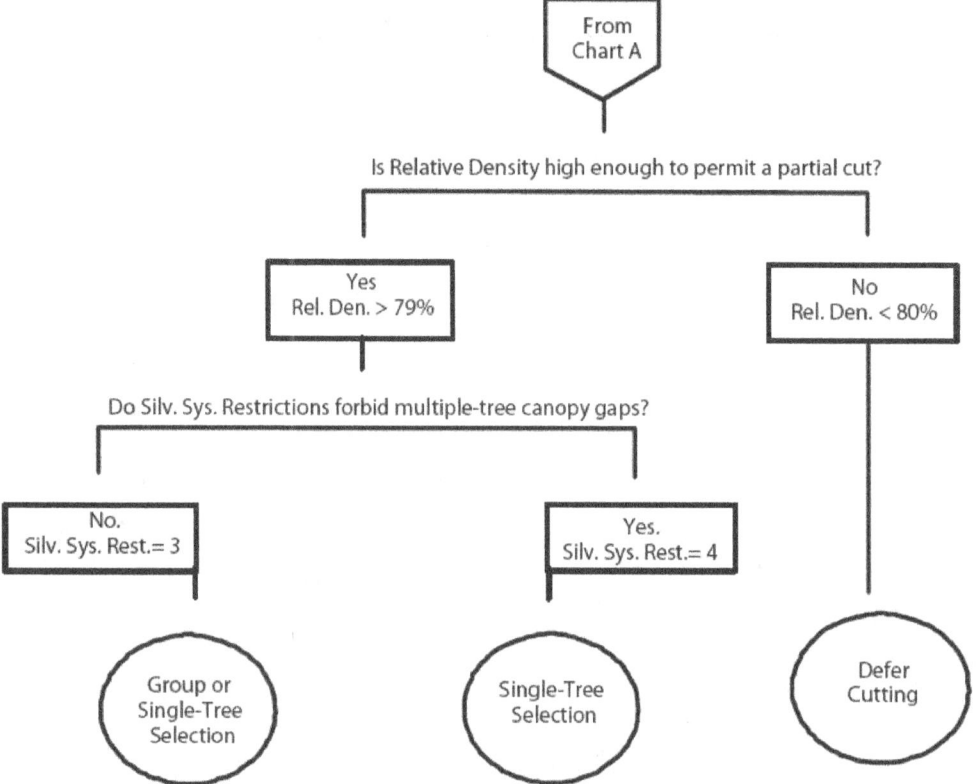

From
Chart A

Is Relative Density high enough to permit a partial cut?

Yes
Rel. Den. > 79%

No
Rel. Den. < 80%

Do Silv. Sys. Restrictions forbid multiple-tree canopy gaps?

No.
Silv. Sys. Rest.= 3

Yes.
Silv. Sys. Rest.= 4

Group or
Single-Tree
Selection

Single-Tree
Selection

Defer
Cutting

# Prescription Type Legend

Prescription

These prescriptions generally produce the desired results and require no investment. We strongly recommend these treatments.

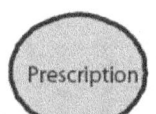
Prescription

These prescriptions are problematic. They require an investment and do not yield an economic return for 5 to 10 years. If such investments meet your organization's economic criteria, we recommend them. If not, we recommend no treatment. In the case of regeneration prescriptions, stands generally will not reproduce without the recommended treatment.

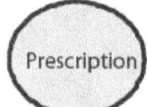
Prescription

These prescriptions generally produce the desired results, require an investment, and usually yield an economic return at the same time. If such investments meet your organization's economic criteria, we recommend them. If not, we recommend no treatment. In the case of regeneration prescriptions, stands generally will not reproduce without the recommended treatment.

Prescription

These prescriptions are problematic. They require an investment with little or no chance of an economic return in the foreseeable future. Stands of this type are difficult to regenerate. We recommend no treatment but if some action is considered necessary, we suggest you consider the treatment shown.

Chart C
Thinning
Prescriptions

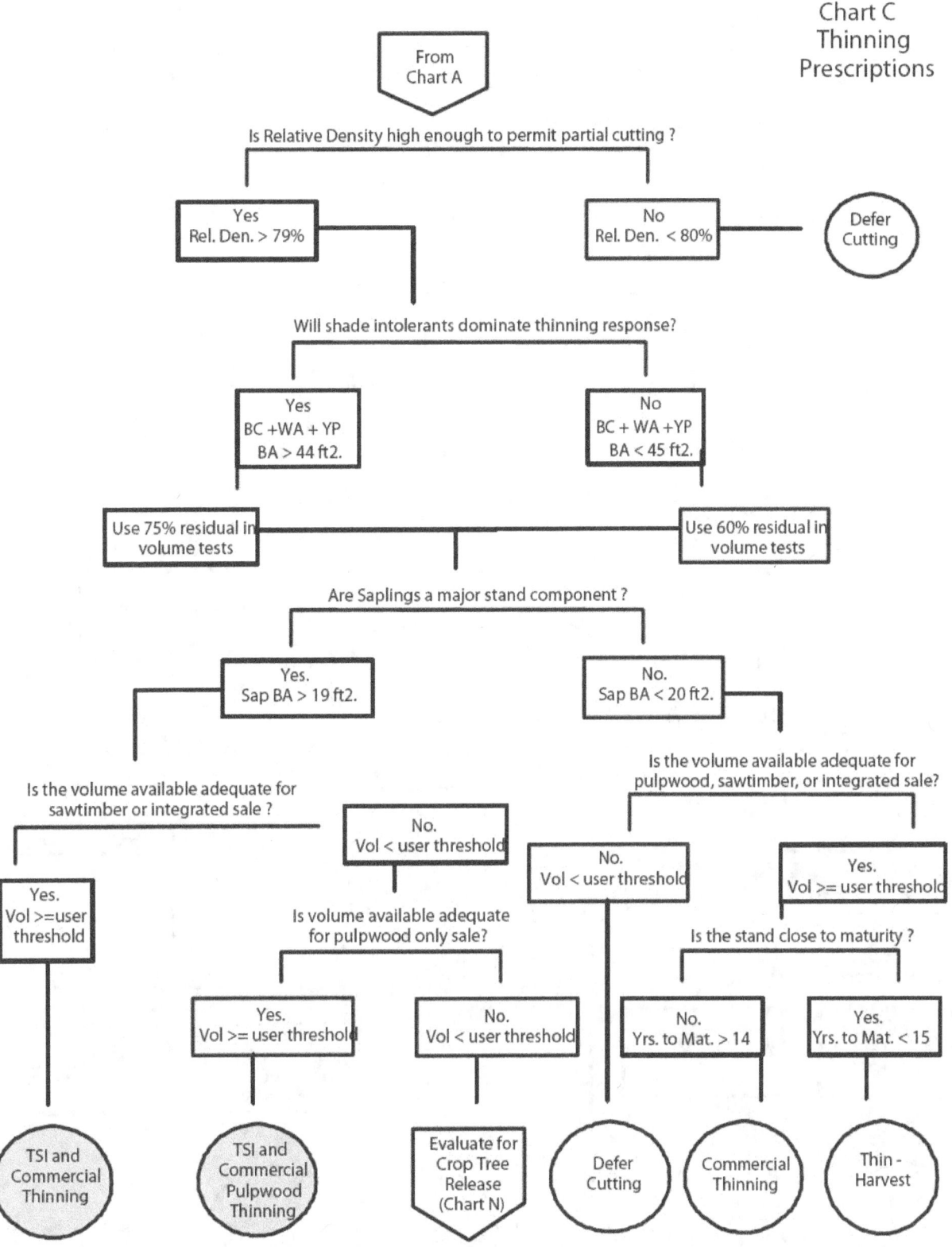

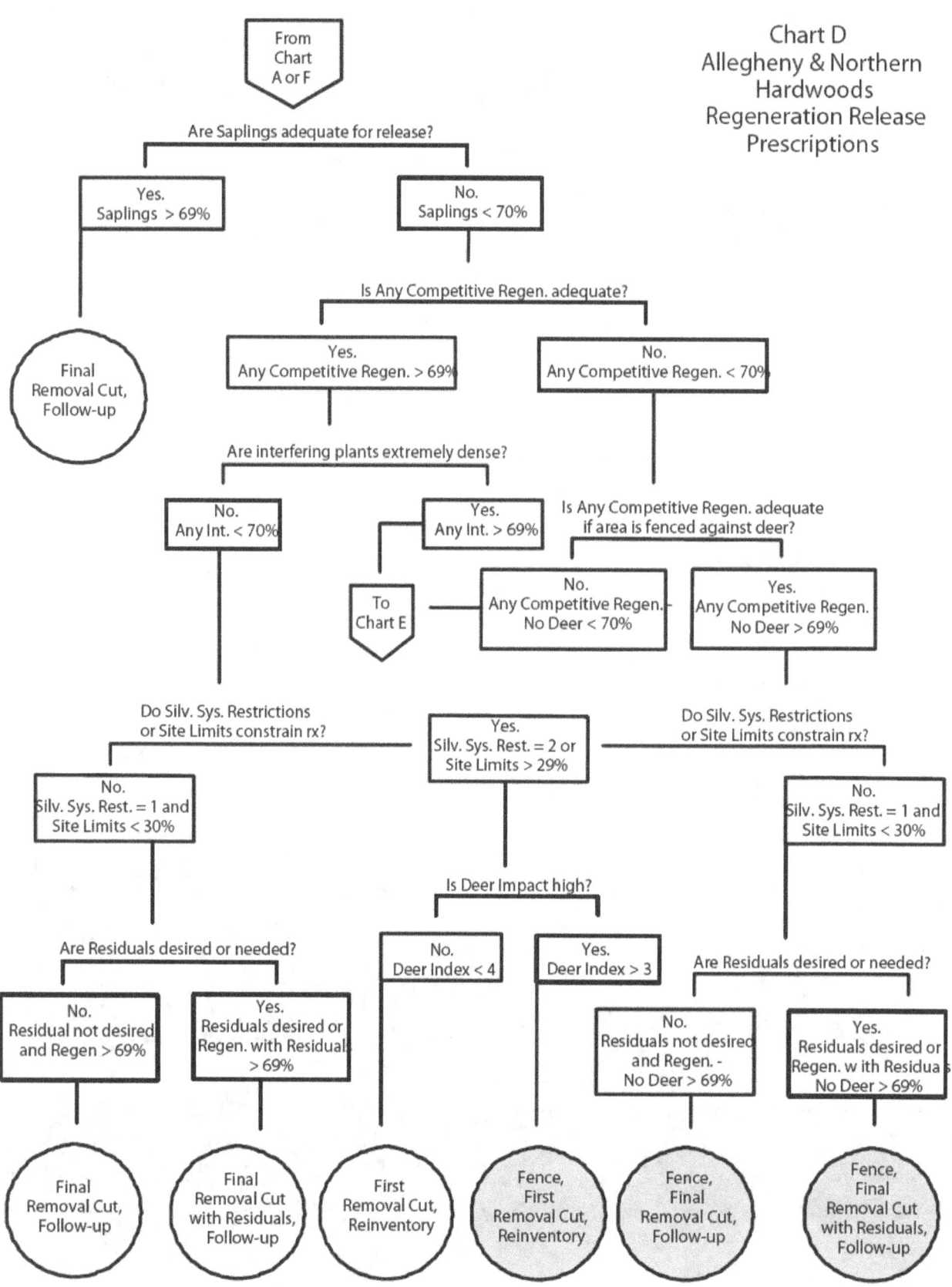

From Chart A or F

Are Saplings adequate for release?

Yes. Saplings > 69%

No. Saplings < 70%

Final Removal Cut, Follow-up

Is Any Competitive Regen. adequate?

Yes. Any Competitive Regen. > 69%

No. Any Competitive Regen. < 70%

Are interfering plants extremely dense?

No. Any Int. < 70%

Yes. Any Int. > 69%

Is Any Competitive Regen. adequate if area is fenced against deer?

To Chart E

No. Any Competitive Regen. - No Deer < 70%

Yes. Any Competitive Regen. No Deer > 69%

Do Silv. Sys. Restrictions or Site Limits constrain rx?

No. Silv. Sys. Rest. = 1 and Site Limits < 30%

Yes. Silv. Sys. Rest. = 2 or Site Limits > 29%

Do Silv. Sys. Restrictions or Site Limits constrain rx?

No. Silv. Sys. Rest. = 1 and Site Limits < 30%

Is Deer Impact high?

Are Residuals desired or needed?

No. Residual not desired and Regen > 69%

Yes. Residuals desired or Regen. with Residual > 69%

No. Deer Index < 4

Yes. Deer Index > 3

Are Residuals desired or needed?

No. Residuals not desired and Regen. - No Deer > 69%

Yes. Residuals desired or Regen. with Residuals No Deer > 69%

Final Removal Cut, Follow-up

Final Removal Cut with Residuals, Follow-up

First Removal Cut, Reinventory

Fence, First Removal Cut, Reinventory

Fence, Final Removal Cut, Follow-up

Fence, Final Removal Cut with Residuals, Follow-up

Chart D
Allegheny & Northern Hardwoods Regeneration Release Prescriptions

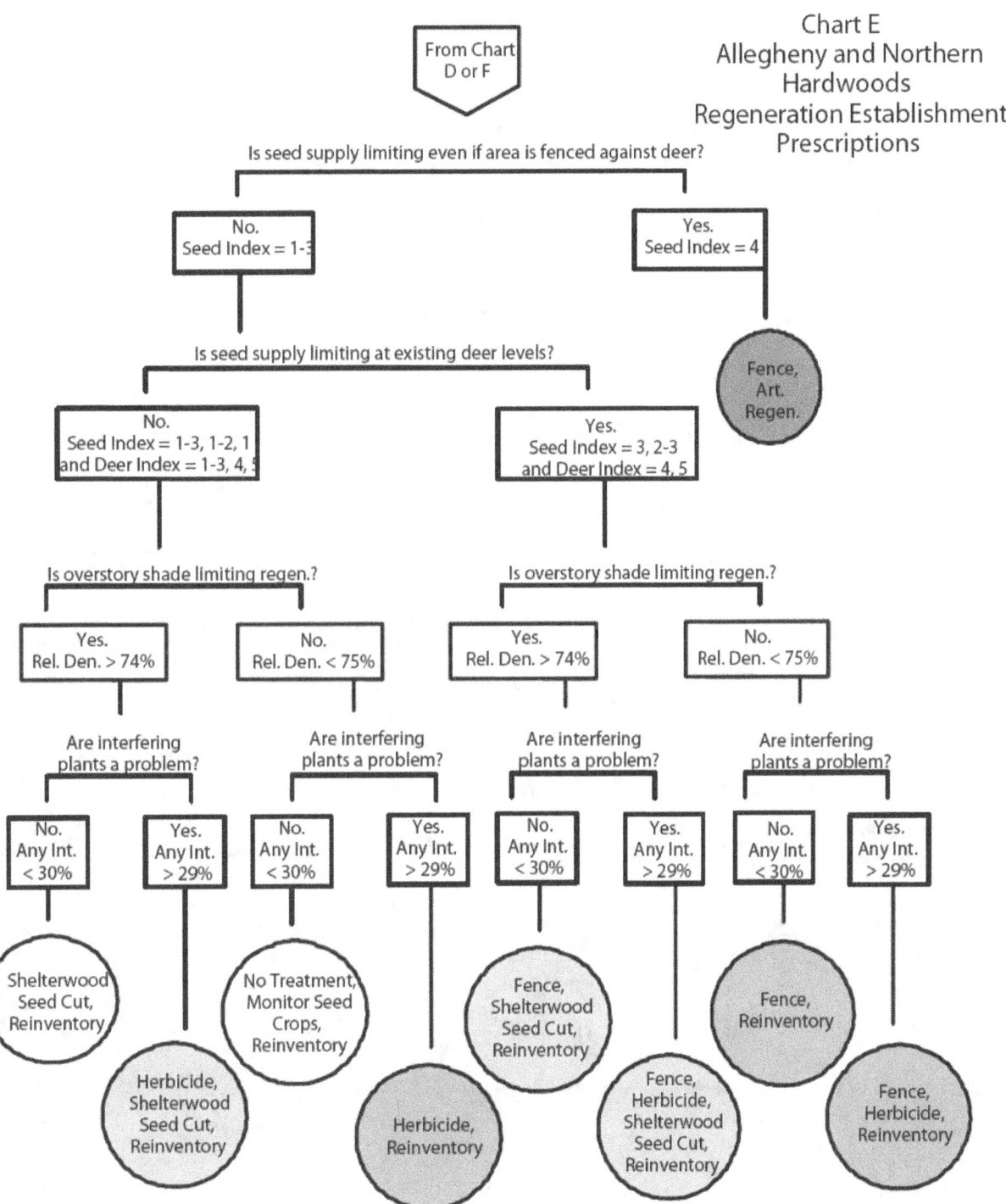

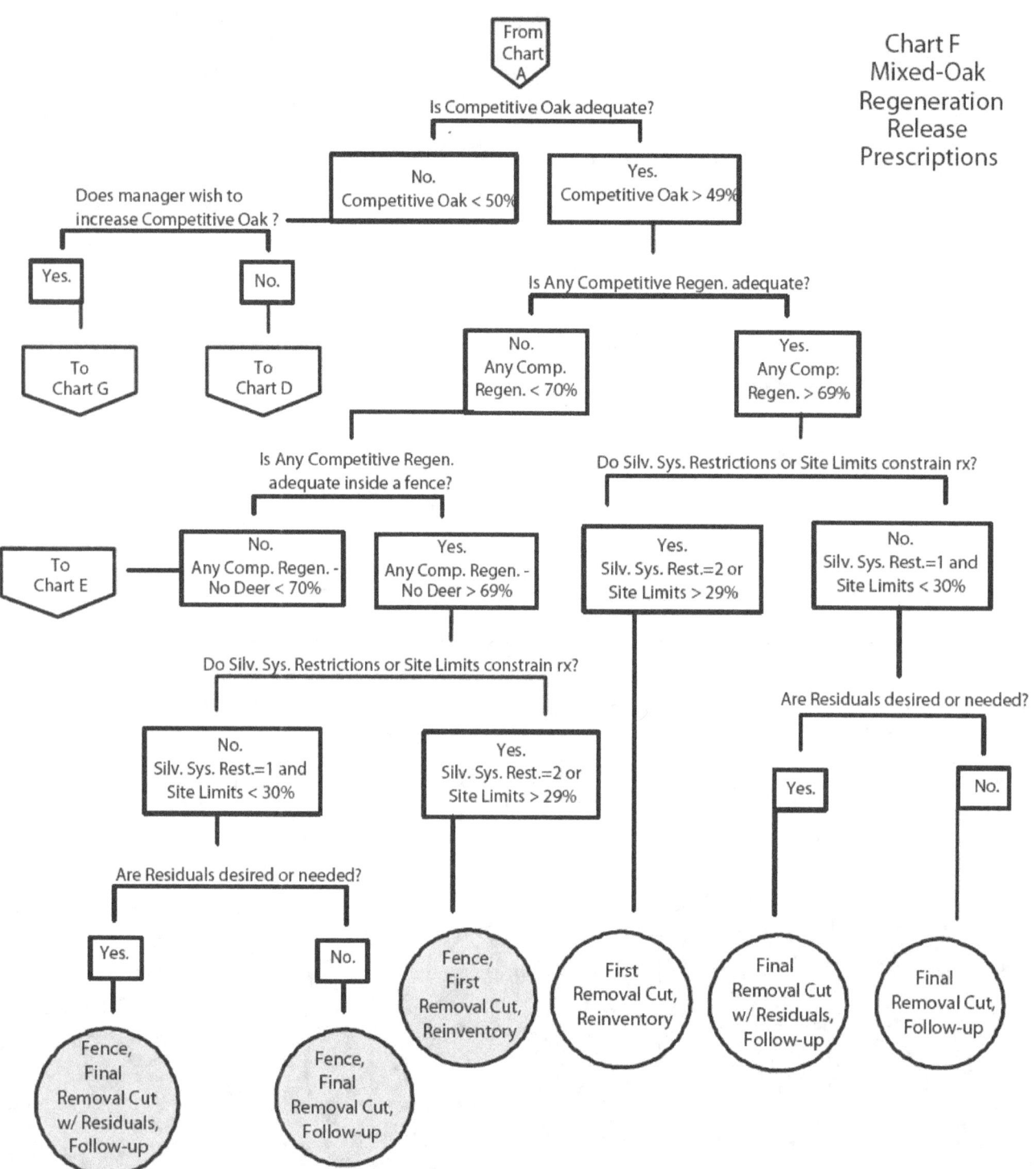

From Chart A

Is Competitive Oak adequate?

No. Competitive Oak < 50%

Yes. Competitive Oak > 49%

Does manager wish to increase Competitive Oak ?

Yes.

No.

To Chart G

To Chart D

Is Any Competitive Regen. adequate?

No. Any Comp. Regen. < 70%

Yes. Any Comp: Regen. > 69%

Is Any Competitive Regen. adequate inside a fence?

Do Silv. Sys. Restrictions or Site Limits constrain rx?

To Chart E

No. Any Comp. Regen. - No Deer < 70%

Yes. Any Comp. Regen. - No Deer > 69%

Yes. Silv. Sys. Rest.=2 or Site Limits > 29%

No. Silv. Sys. Rest.=1 and Site Limits < 30%

Do Silv. Sys. Restrictions or Site Limits constrain rx?

Are Residuals desired or needed?

No. Silv. Sys. Rest.=1 and Site Limits < 30%

Yes. Silv. Sys. Rest.=2 or Site Limits > 29%

Yes.

No.

Are Residuals desired or needed?

Yes.

No.

Fence, Final Removal Cut w/ Residuals, Follow-up

Fence, Final Removal Cut, Follow-up

Fence, First Removal Cut, Reinventory

First Removal Cut, Reinventory

Final Removal Cut w/ Residuals, Follow-up

Final Removal Cut, Follow-up

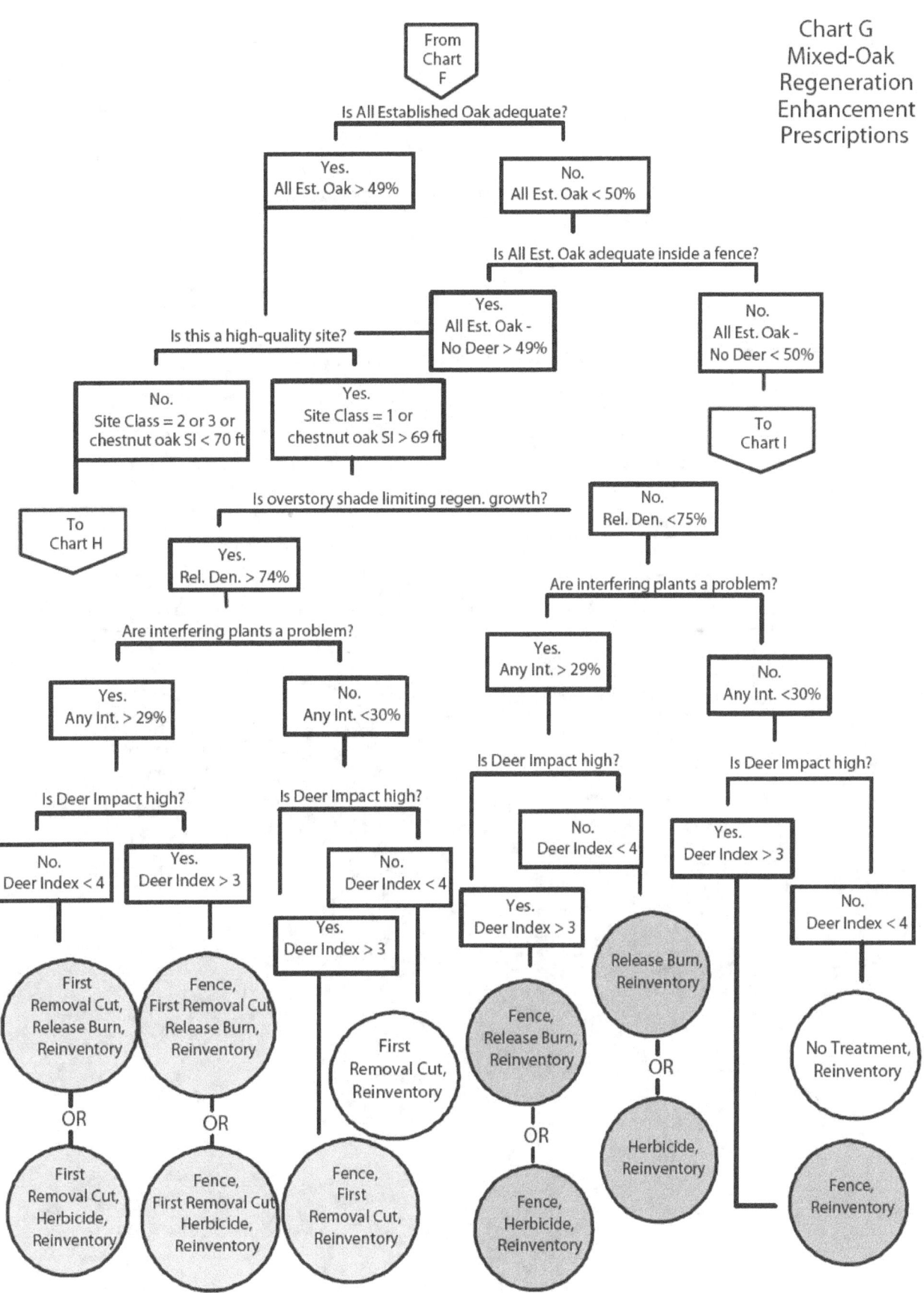

From Chart F

Is All Established Oak adequate?

Yes.
All Est. Oak > 49%

No.
All Est. Oak < 50%

Is All Est. Oak adequate inside a fence?

Yes.
All Est. Oak -
No Deer > 49%

No.
All Est. Oak -
No Deer < 50%

Is this a high-quality site?

No.
Site Class = 2 or 3 or
chestnut oak SI < 70 ft

Yes.
Site Class = 1 or
chestnut oak SI > 69 ft

To
Chart I

To
Chart H

Is overstory shade limiting regen. growth?

No.
Rel. Den. <75%

Yes.
Rel. Den. > 74%

Are interfering plants a problem?

Are interfering plants a problem?

Yes.
Any Int. > 29%

No.
Any Int. <30%

Yes.
Any Int. > 29%

No.
Any Int. <30%

Is Deer Impact high?

Is Deer Impact high?

Is Deer Impact high?

Is Deer Impact high?

No.
Deer Index < 4

Yes.
Deer Index > 3

No.
Deer Index < 4

No.
Deer Index < 4

Yes.
Deer Index > 3

No.
Deer Index < 4

Yes.
Deer Index > 3

Yes.
Deer Index > 3

First
Removal Cut,
Release Burn,
Reinventory

Fence,
First Removal Cut,
Release Burn,
Reinventory

First
Removal Cut,
Reinventory

Fence,
Release Burn,
Reinventory

Release Burn,
Reinventory

No Treatment,
Reinventory

OR

OR

OR

OR

First
Removal Cut,
Herbicide,
Reinventory

Fence,
First Removal Cut,
Herbicide,
Reinventory

Fence,
First
Removal Cut,
Reinventory

Fence,
Herbicide,
Reinventory

Herbicide,
Reinventory

Fence,
Reinventory

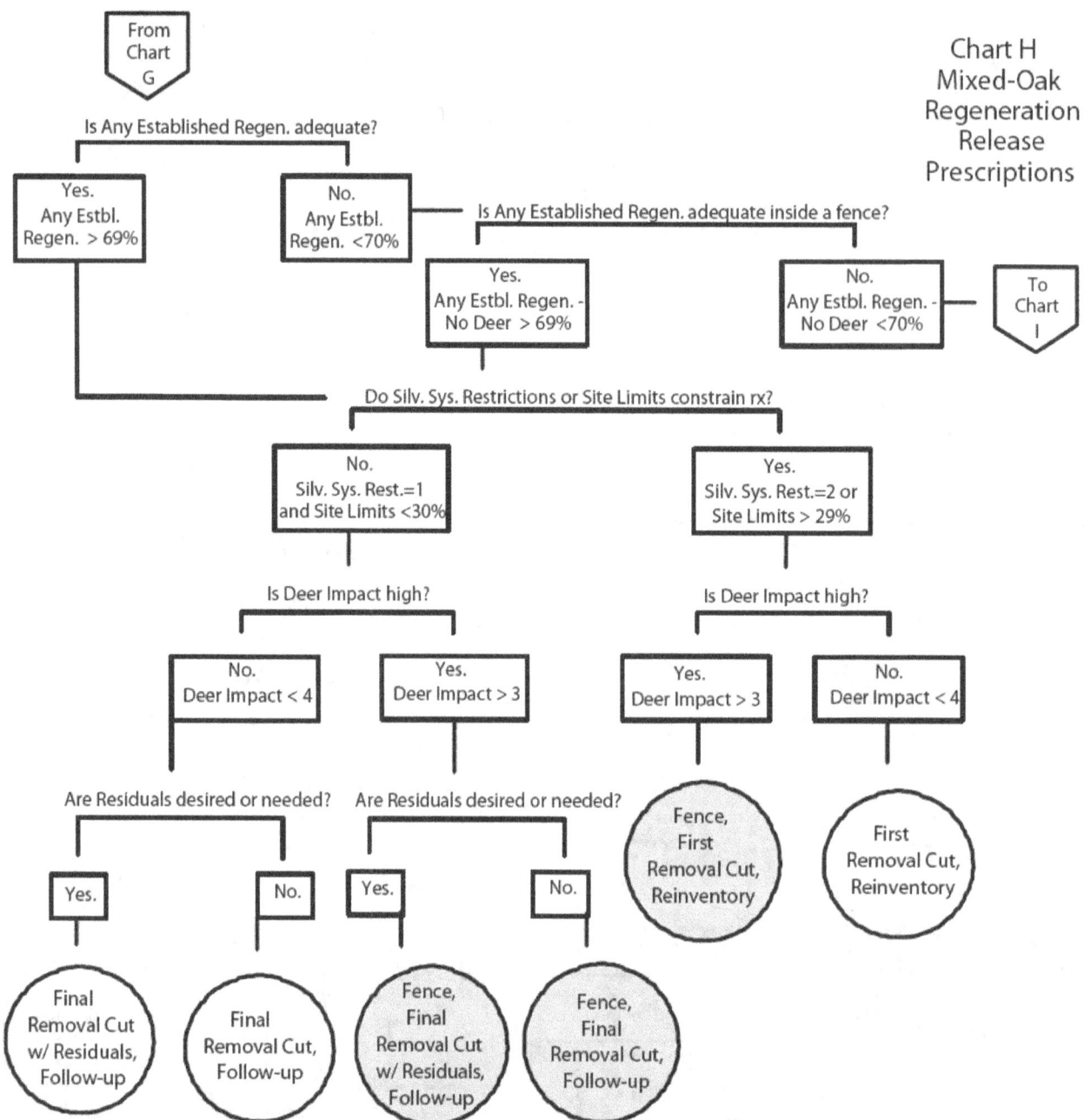

From Chart G

Is Any Established Regen. adequate?

Yes.
Any Estbl.
Regen. > 69%

No.
Any Estbl.
Regen. <70%

Is Any Established Regen. adequate inside a fence?

Yes.
Any Estbl. Regen. -
No Deer > 69%

No.
Any Estbl. Regen. -
No Deer <70%

To Chart I

Do Silv. Sys. Restrictions or Site Limits constrain rx?

No.
Silv. Sys. Rest.=1
and Site Limits <30%

Yes.
Silv. Sys. Rest.=2 or
Site Limits > 29%

Is Deer Impact high?

No.
Deer Impact < 4

Yes.
Deer Impact > 3

Is Deer Impact high?

Yes.
Deer Impact > 3

No.
Deer Impact < 4

Are Residuals desired or needed?

Are Residuals desired or needed?

Yes.

No.

Yes.

No.

Final
Removal Cut
w/ Residuals,
Follow-up

Final
Removal Cut,
Follow-up

Fence,
Final
Removal Cut
w/ Residuals,
Follow-up

Fence,
Final
Removal Cut,
Follow-up

Fence,
First
Removal Cut,
Reinventory

First
Removal Cut,
Reinventory

Chart H
Mixed-Oak
Regeneration
Release
Prescriptions

38

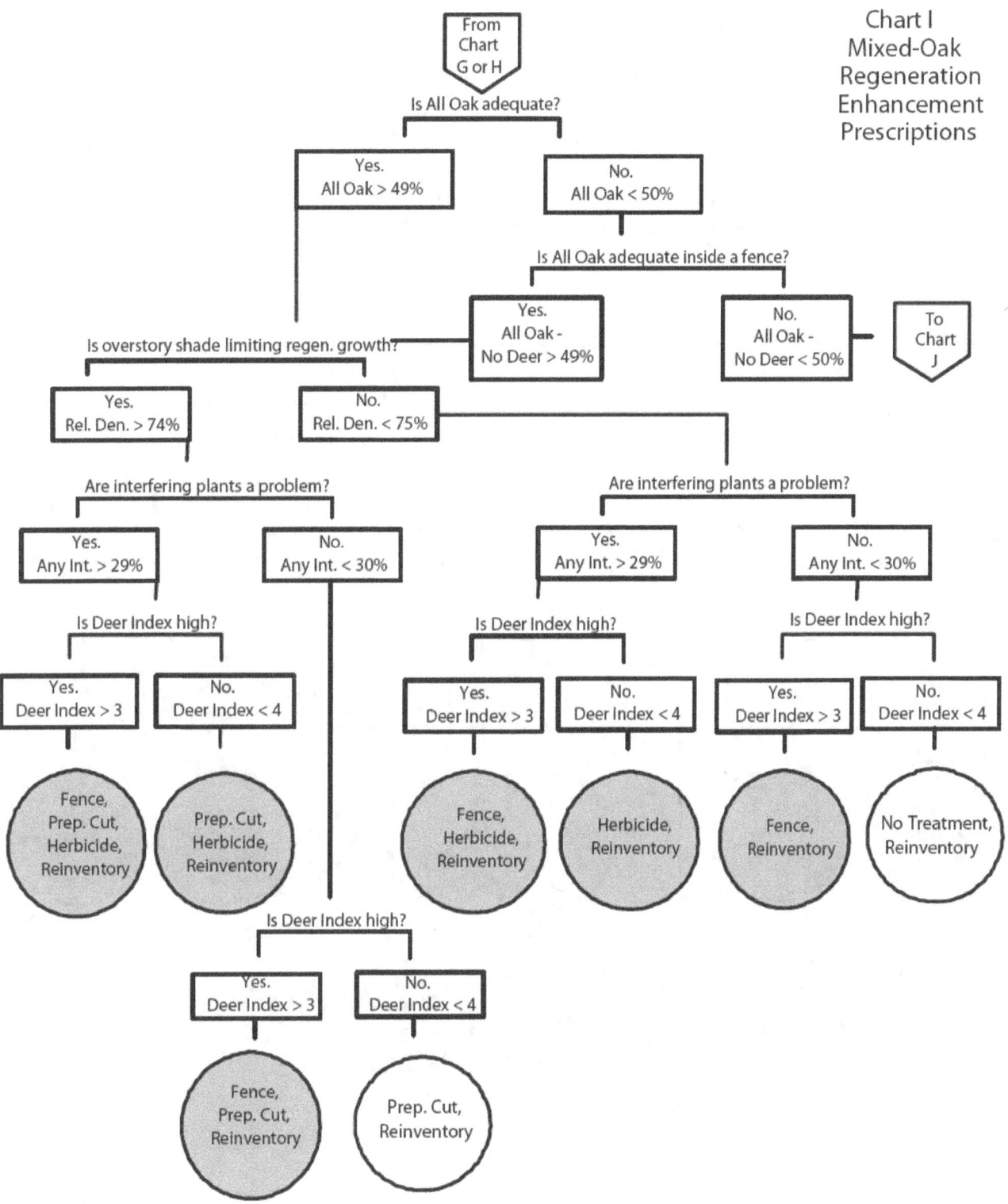

Chart I
Mixed-Oak
Regeneration
Enhancement
Prescriptions

From
Chart
G or H

Is All Oak adequate?

Yes.
All Oak > 49%

No.
All Oak < 50%

Is All Oak adequate inside a fence?

Yes.
All Oak -
No Deer > 49%

No.
All Oak -
No Deer < 50%

To
Chart
J

Is overstory shade limiting regen. growth?

Yes.
Rel. Den. > 74%

No.
Rel. Den. < 75%

Are interfering plants a problem?

Are interfering plants a problem?

Yes.
Any Int. > 29%

No.
Any Int. < 30%

Yes.
Any Int. > 29%

No.
Any Int. < 30%

Is Deer Index high?

Is Deer Index high?

Is Deer Index high?

Yes.
Deer Index > 3

No.
Deer Index < 4

Yes.
Deer Index > 3

No.
Deer Index < 4

Yes.
Deer Index > 3

No.
Deer Index < 4

Fence,
Prep. Cut,
Herbicide,
Reinventory

Prep. Cut,
Herbicide,
Reinventory

Fence,
Herbicide,
Reinventory

Herbicide,
Reinventory

Fence,
Reinventory

No Treatment,
Reinventory

Is Deer Index high?

Yes.
Deer Index > 3

No.
Deer Index < 4

Fence,
Prep. Cut,
Reinventory

Prep. Cut,
Reinventory

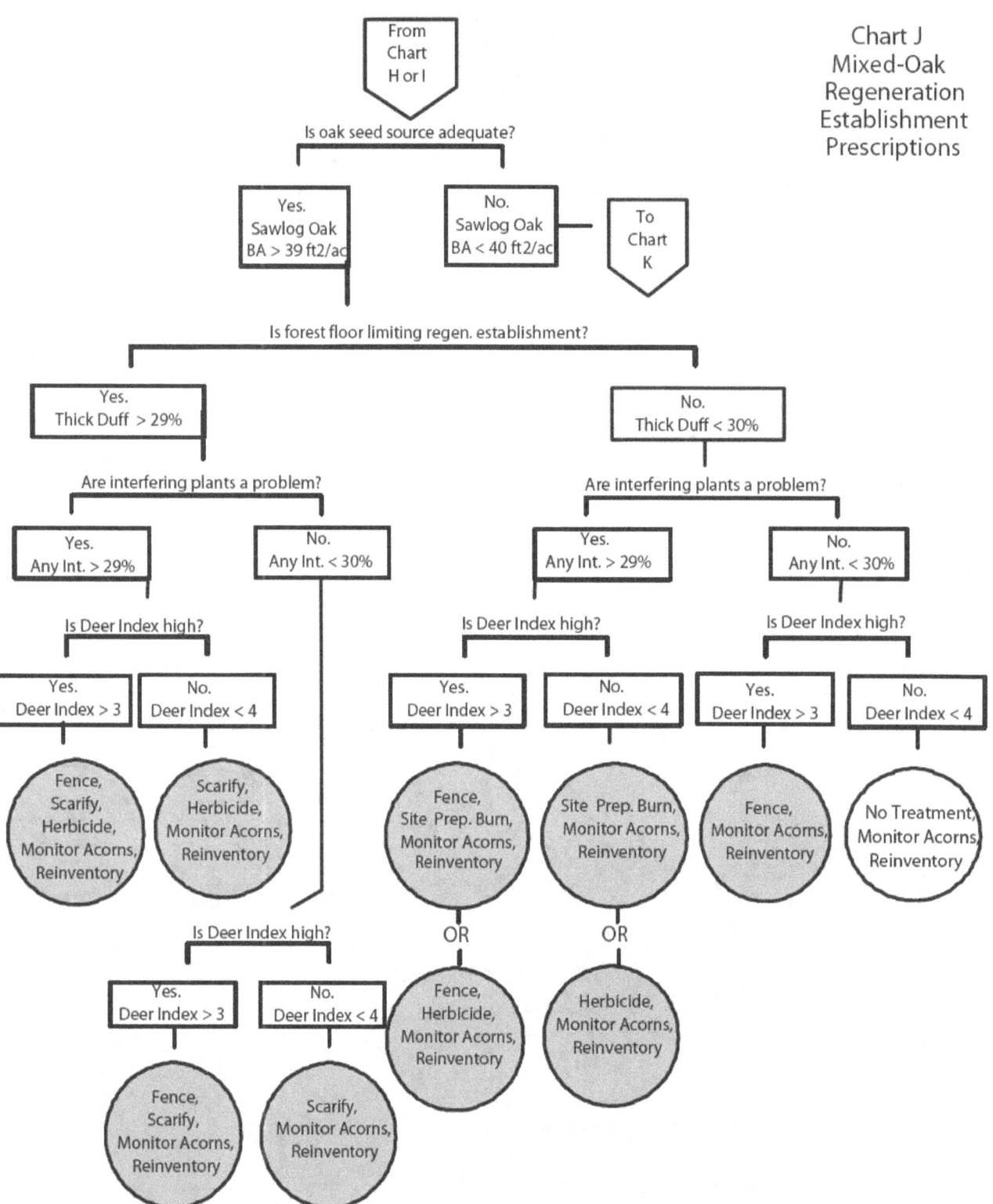

From
Chart
H or I

Chart J
Mixed-Oak
Regeneration
Establishment
Prescriptions

Is oak seed source adequate?

Yes.
Sawlog Oak
BA > 39 ft2/ac

No.
Sawlog Oak
BA < 40 ft2/ac

To
Chart
K

Is forest floor limiting regen. establishment?

Yes.
Thick Duff > 29%

No.
Thick Duff < 30%

Are interfering plants a problem?

Are interfering plants a problem?

Yes.
Any Int. > 29%

No.
Any Int. < 30%

Yes.
Any Int. > 29%

No.
Any Int. < 30%

Is Deer Index high?

Is Deer Index high?

Is Deer Index high?

Yes.
Deer Index > 3

No.
Deer Index < 4

Yes.
Deer Index > 3

No.
Deer Index < 4

Yes.
Deer Index > 3

No.
Deer Index < 4

Fence,
Scarify,
Herbicide,
Monitor Acorns,
Reinventory

Scarify,
Herbicide,
Monitor Acorns,
Reinventory

Fence,
Site Prep. Burn,
Monitor Acorns,
Reinventory

Site Prep. Burn,
Monitor Acorns,
Reinventory

Fence,
Monitor Acorns,
Reinventory

No Treatment,
Monitor Acorns,
Reinventory

OR

OR

Is Deer Index high?

Yes.
Deer Index > 3

No.
Deer Index < 4

Fence,
Herbicide,
Monitor Acorns,
Reinventory

Herbicide,
Monitor Acorns,
Reinventory

Fence,
Scarify,
Monitor Acorns,
Reinventory

Scarify,
Monitor Acorns,
Reinventory

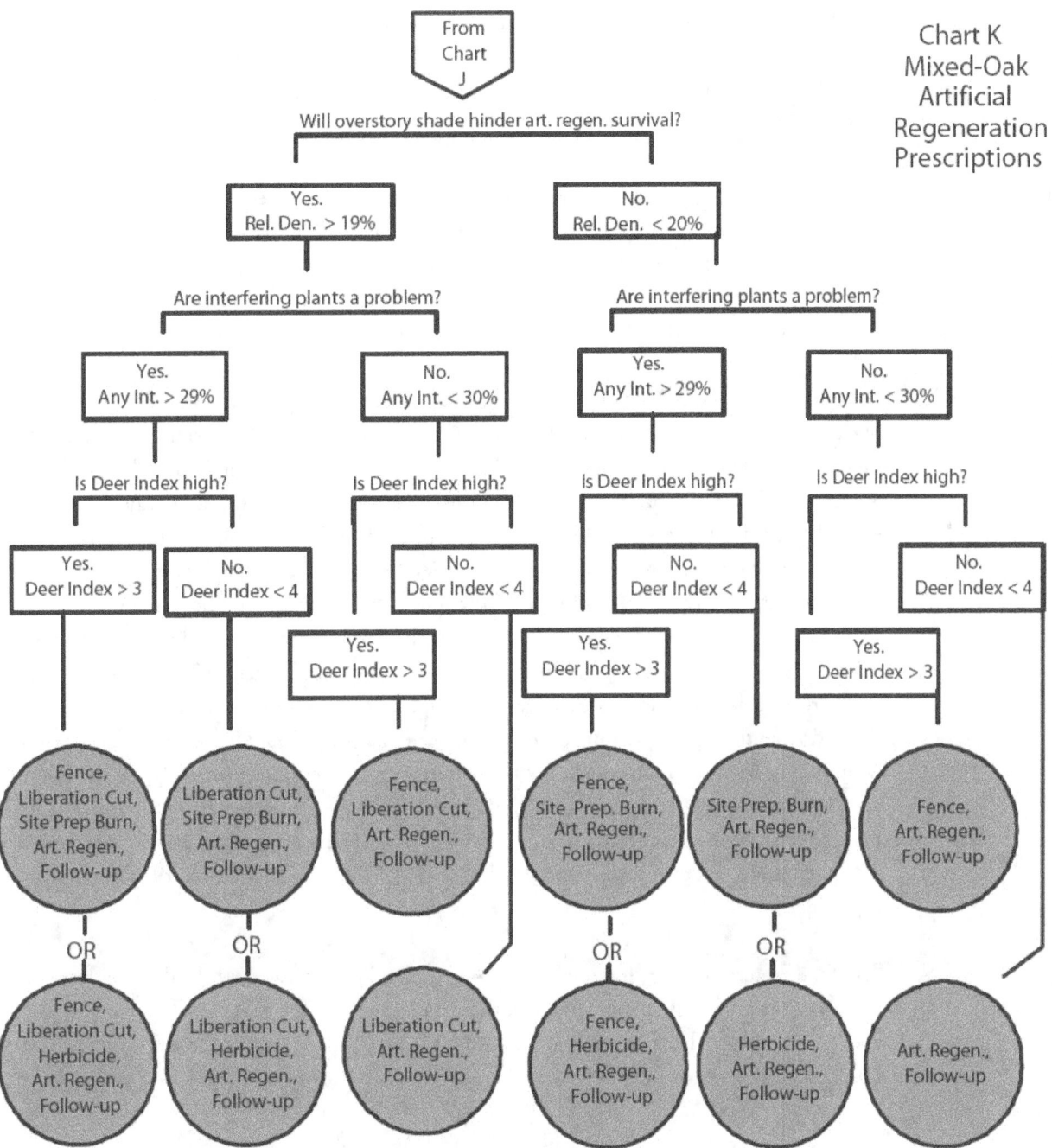

# CHAPTER 5: OAK REGENERATION PRESCRIPTIONS

**Patrick Brose, Kurt Gottschalk, Steve Horsley, Peter Knopp, Jim Kochenderfer, Gary Miller, and Susan Stout**

The goal of the oak prescriptions in this guidebook is to create, directly or indirectly, new even-aged hardwood stands with oak as at least 50 percent of the dominant and codominant trees at canopy closure (age 10 to 20, depending on site quality). At this point in stand development, crop tree management (Chapter 6) is appropriate to shape species composition of the stand and ensure long-term survival of the selected crop trees.

Each SILVAH printout (Appendix 3) contains a prescription of one or more silvicultural practices from a variety of sources. Those on Charts B - E are from "Prescribing Silvicultural Treatments in Hardwood Stands of the Alleghenies" (revised) by Marquis and others (1992). Some of the oak-prescription practices are from other forest types within this region. For example, broadcast spraying of herbicide to control ferns is from research conducted in Allegheny and northern hardwood forests (Horsley 1981, 1989, 1990; Horsley and others 1992) but also is effective in oak forests. Other prescriptions are from other regions where their effectiveness has been documented. For example, the herbicide-shelterwood method of Loftis (1985, 1990) and the shelterwood-burn technique of Brose and others (1999a, b) are from the Southern Appalachian and Piedmont regions, respectively. They are currently being tested in the mid-Atlantic region; preliminary results indicate that they would be effective in this region with minor revisions to account for local circumstances. Others treatments, e.g., scarification, are from research results (Zaczek and others 1997) that have never been incorporated into a management technique. Many prescriptions contain a fencing recommendation, a practice that is as much the result of formal research (Marquis 1977, Marquis and Grisez 1978) as hands-on experience.

All of the prescriptions are founded on the two cardinal rules of successful oak silviculture: 1) there must be competitive sources of oak regeneration in advance of the final overstory harvest, and 2) that advanced oak regeneration must be adequately and timely released (Loftis 2004). Ignoring these cardinal rules likely will result in an oak regeneration failure.

These two rules contain the following caveats that are equally as important:
1) Regenerating oaks becomes more problematic as site quality improves. Once oak site index exceeds 65 feet (an intermediate site), competition from other vegetation becomes intense and it is difficult to regenerate an oak forest (Lorimer 1993).
2) High densities of small oak seedlings are necessary to obtain large oak advanced regeneration on high-quality sites because of substantial oak mortality rates (Loftis 1990a; Miller and others 2004a).
3) The key to growing small oak seedlings to large oak advanced regeneration is to manage their root development by controlling understory shade and protecting from deer browsing (Miller and others 2004a, Brose 2008).

Because of these caveats, regenerating oak stands, especially on high-quality sites, is a process, not an event. Several years are required to implement a two-practice prescription and a decade or more likely would be required to complete a prescription of three or more practices.

## Fencing

There are three fence types: electric, plastic, and woven wire (Fig. 5.1). Of these, only the woven-wire fence should be used in oak forests as it likely will be in place for a decade. Fence height should be a minimum of 8 feet and the bottom of the fence must be anchored flush to the ground, especially in low spots. Fence layout should be oval to rectangular, without acute interior angles, and no larger than 50 acres. Experience shows that deer readily move around these types of fences with minimal penetration. If the area to be fenced exceeds 50 acres, construct two or more fences with travel corridors between them. Once the fence is erected, drive the entire stand and remove any deer that are inside the fence. The fence will require at least monthly inspections and occasional maintenance.

In some cases when deer impact is level 3 (moderate), there may be alternatives to fencing. On large land ownerships (more than 1 square mile) on which there has been little or no hunting, an aggressive hunting program targeted at does and sustained throughout the regeneration process may reduce browsing pressure enough to allow regeneration to grow beyond the reach of deer. In this scenario, defer harvesting until deer impact is reduced substantially. Another approach is leaving as much logging slash as possible in the stand after a harvest to protect the regeneration from deer.

Figure 5.1.—Deer exclusion fences are electric or are made of plastic or woven-wire.

## Final Removal Cut

The final removal cut is the last harvest of a regeneration sequence. The cut creates a high light environment that favors both growth of the competitive oak regeneration already in place and the reproduction of shade-intolerant hardwoods (Fig. 5.2). To implement this practice, harvest all trees larger than 1-inch d.b.h. In rare cases where a sapling layer of oak species is present, harvest the overstory carefully to minimize damage to the oak saplings. As much as 15 ft$^2$ basal area of residual trees can be left post-harvest to meet aesthetic, diversity, or wildlife objectives.

## First Removal Cut

The first removal cut is the first harvest in a shelterwood sequence **after** the oak regeneration is present and established (Smith 1986). It creates a suitable understory light regime that allows established oak regeneration to develop into the competitive size class within several years (Brose 2008). Reduce overstory stocking to between 40 and 60-percent relative density, depending on site qulity (Fig. 5.3). Retain sufficient merchantable trees so that a seed source is maintained on site. This ensures that acorns will be available in the future if the existing oak advanced regeneration is somehow destroyed. It also provides a second commercial harvest within 5 to 10 years. Retain any pole-size trees that may be needed as long-term residuals to meet aesthetic, diversity, or wildlife objectives.

## Herbicide

Herbicide is an effective, safe and economical technique for removing vegetation that interferes with establishment and growth of oak regeneration. There are five different application techniques for using herbicides to control interfering vegetation (Fig. 5.4). Each is matched with a specific set of conditions where it will provide effective control. With all, be sure to follow all instructions on the herbicide label, wear appropriate safety clothing and equipment, and follow applicable laws with regard to herbicide applicator licensing.

Photo by Patrick Brose, Northern Research Station

Figure 5.2.—The final removal cut finishes the regeneration sequence and creates conditions of full sunlight required by shade-intolerant and shade-intermediate species.

Photo by Patrick Brose, Northern Research Station

Figure 5.3.—The first removal cut of a shelterwood sequence reduces overstory relative density to about 50 percent. This level is sufficient for the timely development of oak seedling root systems.

1) **Broadcast Spray.** Use this technique to prepare the forest understory for the establishment of desirable regeneration. Broadcast spraying generally is done with mechanized equipment because large areas, i.e., several acres or more, are sprayed at one time, but small areas can be treated with a backpack sprayer. The height of the effective spray zone is from the forest floor to about 15 feet, depending on the equipment. Two principal herbicides are labeled for broadcast spray operations on silvicultural sites, glyphosate and sulfometuron methyl (Horsley 1991). Glyphosate is a broad spectrum herbicide that controls many herbaceous and woody plant species. Addition of a non-ionic surfactant is required when using glyphosate. However, species with waxy leaf

Photos by Steve Horsley and Jim Kochenderfer, Northern Research Station

Figure 5.4.—Herbicide strategies include broadcast and individual stem treatments.

coatings (mountain laurel, *Rhododendron* spp.) are either poorly controlled at the rate we recommend or not controlled at all. Time of application and complete coverage of target species are important for optimum vegetation control at our recommended rate of 1 - 1.5 pounds of active ingredient per acre in 25 gallons of water. Grasses and sedges are best controlled with application made between early June and mid-September; fern (particularly hay-scented and New York) control is best between early July and mid-September; understory trees of striped maple and beech are best controlled between early August and mid-September. Complete coverage of striped maple crowns is particularly important for good control. Glyphosate has no soil residual activity, so seeds in the forest floor seed bank are unaffected. Drought diminishes the efficacy of glyphosate, particularly on ferns and striped maple, because drought reduces absorption and translocation of herbicide. Under these circumstances, it is important to suspend herbicide application until there has been enough rainfall to return plants to active growth.

Sulfometuron methyl is a selective herbicide that controls some herbaceous and woody plants. Unlike glyphosate, sulfometuron methyl has a short-term soil residual activity that reduces emergence of grasses and sedges germinating from seed and fern not killed by the aboveground spray. This is called pre-emergent soil activity. Ferns are well controlled by sulfometuron methyl, but the mature plants of many grass and sedge species are not; neither striped maple nor beech is controlled by sulfometuron methyl. Sulfometuron methyl can be used to prepare a stand for establishment of desirable regeneration or to release new and established oak seedlings from interference by susceptible species. Northern red oak and white oak are not damaged by overspray of the recommended rate of sulfometuron methyl application, 1.5 ounces of active ingredient per acre in 25 gallons of water. Regeneration of some hardwood species are sensitive to sulfometuron methyl if spraying is conducted in early summer, but are less sensitive if the herbicide is applied later in the growing season (Horsley and others 1992). For site preparation, sulfometuron methyl often is mixed with glyphosate using the timing constraints suggested for glyphosate. To release new and established oak seedlings from interfering ferns and reduce emergence of grasses and sedges from the seed bank, spray sulfometuron methyl in late summer and **do not use a surfactant**.

2) **Cut and Spray.** Use this method to circumvent the susceptibility of oak regeneration to glyphosate when competitive oak regeneration is intermixed with undesirable woody species (Deen and others 1993). Clip off about 200 competitive oak and other desirable stems per acre throughout the stand at ground level in late summer. The "stubs" of the severed stems will seal the wound within several days, preventing entry of the herbicide into the roots. Once that occurs, broadcast spray a glyphosate herbicide throughout the stand at the previously prescribed rate and time to control interfering vegetation. The stubs of competitive oak and other desirable regeneration will sprout vigorously the following spring, grow rapidly, and become the dominant stems in the new regeneration layer.

3) **Stem Injection.** Use this technique to control individual woody species that are larger than 2 inches d.b.h. and are not suitable, e.g., too tall, growing on a steep hillside, for control by broadcast spraying (Kochenderfer and others 2004). Inject each stem with a 50-percent solution of a glyphosate herbicide at the rates of one injection per inch of d.b.h. and 1 to 2 milliliters of solution per injection. Space the injections evenly around the entire stem. Apply herbicide from July through September, but avoid dry periods as this diminishes the effectiveness of the herbicide.

4) **Basal Application.** Another individual-stem technique used to control woody interference, especially stems less than 2 inches d.b.h. (Kochenderfer and others 2004). To apply this approach, completely coat the lower 12 to 15 inches of each undesirable stem with a 5- to 10- percent solution of a trichlopyr herbicide in an appropriate oil carrier. This type of herbicide can be applied so long as the target stem is not wet or frozen. It is ineffective in controlling thick-barked species such as blackgum or stems more than 6 inches d.b.h.

5) **Cut Stump.** A third individual-stem technique useful for controlling woody interference, especially species that are resilient sprouters (Kochenderfer and others 2006). This two-step method entails chainsaw felling of the target stem at ground level followed by application of at least a 50-percent glyphosate herbicide solution to the stump. Felling must be done in the summer or fall and theherbicide applied within an hour of cutting. On stumps less than 6 inches in diameter, treat the entire cut surface. On stumps larger than this diameter, treat only the outer 3 inches of the stump.

## Liberation Cut

This practice is useful in rehabilitating a degraded stand (Fig. 5.5). It entails removing older, less desirable trees that are overtopping desirable young trees. Implement this practice by cutting or killing undesirable and poor-quality trees from all canopy positions until the relative density of the stand is less than 20 percent. The harvest may or may not be commercial depending on the condition of the cut trees. Concentrate the liberation cut on portions of the stand where there already is vigorous desirable regeneration so that it can take advantage of the release.

## Preparatory Cut

This practice is the first harvest in a three-step shelterwood sequence. The objective of this treatment is to remove undesirable species, seed sources of aggressive competitors, and poorly formed stems; thereby providing more growing space for desirable trees that will produce the seed that eventually regenerates the stand (Fig. 5.6). Harvest trees from suppressed, intermediate, and weak codominant crown positions until the relative density reaches approximately 70 percent. Do not harvest oaks that are good acorn producers or create large gaps in the main canopy. With these constraints, this cut may or may not be commercial depending on local markets. In noncommercial situations, this treatment often is accomplished with an individual-stem herbicide technique.

## Release Burn

This type of prescribed fire is used to free competitive oak from competition by other desirable regeneration and interfering woody vegetation (Fig. 5.7). Fire will select for the oak and against the other woody species to varying degrees based on root characteristics (Brose and Van Lear 1998, 2004). Burning can be done after the first removal cut of a shelterwood sequence or after the final removal cut. In either case, wait until the height growth of the competitive oak regeneration begins to fall behind that of the other woody species by more than 2 feet. If there are valuable residual trees, remove slash and other fuel accumulations from the base of the trees to prevent fire damage.

Release burning is done in mid to late spring. In Pennsylvania, this is mid-April to mid-May. Phenologically, the burning window is from bud swelling on the non-oak

Photo by Patrick Brose, Northern Research Station

Figure 5.5.—Liberation cuts are used to rehabilitate degraded stands by removing older, less desirable trees that are overtopping desirable young trees.

Photo by Patrick Brose, Northern Research Station

Figure 5.6.—Preparatory cuts are the first harvest of a three-step shelterwood sequence. They increase growing space for desirable overstory trees by removing undesirable trees from the midstory and raise understory light slightly for the benefit of the oak seedlings.

Photo by Patrick Brose, Northern Research Station

Figure 5.7.—Release burns free established and competitive oak regeneration of competition from other woody species. They are conducted in the spring, during or after a shelterwood sequence, and typically at moderate to high intensity.

hardwoods to full leaf expansion of the canopy trees. The later in this window that burning occurs, the more advantageous for the oak regeneration. Generally, the fire should be moderate to high intensity with flame lengths of more than 2 feet to ensure complete topkill of the understory layer.

## Scarification

This practice prepares a suitable seedbed for oak seedling establishment from acorns (Fig. 5.8). Use heavy equipment such as a bulldozer with a brush rake or root rake or a farm tractor with a heavy disk to disturb the forest floor, disrupt the mat of organic matter, expose mineral soil, and mix the organic matter and soil. Scarify in the fall only when an acorn crop is imminent or has just fallen. Treat at least half of the stand. If there is no acorn crop, do not scarify.

Photo by Jim Zazcek, Southern Illinois University

Figure 5.8.—Scarification prepares a seedbed for acorns and the subsequent establishment of oak seedlings.

## Site Preparation Burn

This type of prescribed fire prepares an oak stand for eventual oak seedling establishment after a future acorn crop (Fig. 5.9). The objective is to reduce dense understory shade and litter loadings so that a larger proportion of an acorn crop successfully germinates and becomes seedlings. Burning can be done in the dormant season (fall or early spring) or growing season (late spring) and at any intensity. However, high-intensity fires (flame lengths greater than 2 feet) in the late spring decrease dense understory shade more quickly than low intensity fires in the fall or early spring. Generally, multiple fires spread over several years are necessary to reduce dense understory shade to a level that improves the survival and growth of new oak seedlings. Do not burn if an acorn crop has just fallen or if new oak seedlings from a recent acorn crop are needed to help regenerate the stand as fire kills acorns and small oak seedlings (Auchmoody and Smith 1993).

Photo by Patrick Brose, Northern Research Station

Figure 5.9.—Site preparation burning prepares a seedbed for eventual oak seedling establishment after a future acorn crop. These burns are done before harvesting, conducted in the spring or fall, and typically are of low intensity.

## Chart F Prescriptions

Chart F prescriptions are for oak stands on high-quality sites. They are at the point in the oak regeneration process at which the competitive oak seedlings need an adequate release so they can begin forming a new stand. Three prescriptions on Chart F include only a final removal cut or a first removal cut if site limitations or the silvicultural system restrictions does not allow for a single complete harvest. They are highly recommended because they produce an income with little cost.

Depending on current conditions, three prescriptions recommend fencing to address problems posed by deer. We advise caution with these prescriptions because they require a cost. If the cost is acceptable to the landowner, the prescriptions are recommended.

If the fencing cost is unacceptable, we recommend no cutting as the browsing pressure by deer likely will result in a regeneration failure. In that case, the landowner needs to re-evaluate his or her desire to increase the oak component of the regeneration pool, consider regenerating other species, and consult prescriptions from Charts D or E.

**Final Removal Cut, Follow-up**

This prescription is appropriate for stands with adequate advanced oak regeneration in the form of competitive oak seedlings or saplings. At least 70 percent of the regeneration plots should be stocked with competitive seedlings of any desirable species, and 50-percent stocked with competitive oak. White-tailed deer should not pose severe problems, i.e., Deer Impact Index less than 4, and there are no visual or site limitations that would preclude complete overstory removal, i.e., no restrictions on clearcutting, and/or site limitations in less than 30 percent of the interference plots

See the Final Removal Cut description for an explanation of how to implement this harvest. About five years after the cut, do a follow-up examination (Chapter 6) of the stand to determine whether oaks in the new stand require release or if problems have developed with respect to deer or interfering vegetation.

**Final Removal Cut with Residuals, Follow-up**

This prescription is appropriate for the same conditions described previously and is implemented in the identical manner except that some trees are retained as residuals for aesthetic, diversity, or wildlife purposes. See the Final Removal Cut description for instructions related to the harvest. For residuals, leave no more than 10 to 15 ft$^2$ of basal area per acre of pole-size trees (6 to 12 inches d.b.h.) with healthy crowns and clean, straight boles free of branches for at least the first 17 feet. Over time, these residuals will be incorporated into the canopy of the new stand. About five years after the cut, do a follow-up examination (Chapter 6) of the stand to determine whether oaks in the new stand require release or if problems have developed with respect to deer or interfering vegetation.

A variation on retention of residuals is two-age management (Fig.5.10; Miller and others 2004b, 2006). In this approach, 10 to 15 ft$^2$ of basal area per acre are retained in medium and large, sawlog-size trees (more than 18 inches d.b.h.). Over time, these large trees form a superdominant component in the new stand.

**Fence, Final Removal Cut, Follow-up**

Stands requiring this prescription have the same key characteristics as those for a Final Removal Cut except that fencing is needed due to extensive browsing by white-tailed deer. See the Final Removal Cut and Fencing for a detailed description of these practices. The fence can be constructed before or after the final harvest. If constructed afterward, it must be built before the start of the first postharvest growing season to protect new stump sprouts. About 5 years after the cut, do a follow-up examination (Chapter 6) of the stand to determine whether oaks in the new stand require release or if problems have developed with respect to deer or interfering vegetation.

**Fence, Final Removal Cut with Residuals, Follow-up**

Stands requiring this prescription have the same key characteristics as those for a Final Removal Cut with Residuals except that fencing is needed due to extensive browsing by white-tailed deer. See the Final Removal Cut and Fencing for a detailed description of these practices. The fence can be constructed before or after the final harvest. If constructed afterward, it must be erected before the start of the first postharvest growing season to protect new stump sprouts. For residuals, leave no more than 10 to 15 ft$^2$ of basal area per acre of pole-size trees (6 to 12 inches d.b.h.) with healthy crowns and clean, straight boles free of branches for at least the first 17 feet. Over time, these residuals will be incorporated into the canopy of the new stand. About 5 years after the cut, do a follow-up examination (Chapter 6) of the stand to determine whether oaks in the new stand require release or if problems have developed with respect to deer or interfering vegetation.

A variation on retention of residuals is two-age management (Fig.5.10; Miller and others 2004b, 2006). In this approach, 10 to 15 ft$^2$ of basal area per acre is retained in medium and large, sawlog-size trees (more than 18 inches d.b.h.). Over time, these large trees form a superdominant component in the new stand.

Photo by Gary Miller, Northern Research Station

Figure 5.10.—Two-age management retains trees larger than 18 inches d.b.h. to meet visual constraints or ameloriate limitations such as an elevated water table or thin soil.

**First Removal Cut, Reinventory**

This prescription is recommended when visual or site limitations preclude a final removal cut, i.e. there are restrictions on clearcutting and/or site limitations in more than 30 percent of the interference plots. Retaining mature trees protects the young regeneration from desiccation on dry, rocky sites as well as from inundation on wetter sites with poorly drained soils. Otherwise, this prescription is the same as the Final Removal Cut in that at least 70 percent of the regeneration plots are stocked with competitive seedlings of any desirable species, and 50 percent are stocked with competitive oak. Interfering vegetation and white-tailed deer do not pose a problem. This prescription should yield a financial return.

See the First Removal Cut for a detailed description concerning this practice. About five years after the cut, do a complete SILVAH inventory (Chapter 2) of the stand to determine whether competitive oaks are ready for the final harvest and if problems have developed with respect to deer and interfering vegetation.

**Fence, First Removal Cut, Reinventory**

Stands requiring this prescription have the same key characteristics as those for a First Removal Cut except that fencing is needed due to extensive browsing by white-tailed deer. See the First Removal Cut and Fencing for detailed descriptions concerning these practices. The fence can be constructed before or after the harvest. If constructed afterward, it must be erected before the start of the first postharvest growing season to protect new stump sprouts. About five years after the cut, do a complete SILVAH inventory (Chapter 2) of the stand to determine whether competitive oaks are ready for the final harvest and if problems have developed with respect to deer and interfering vegetation.

## Chart G Prescriptions

Chart G prescriptions are for oak stands on high quality sites. These prescriptions are applied about midway through the oak-regeneration process and are designed to promote the development of smaller oak regeneration into the competitive size class, eventually setting the stage for a future final harvest. We advise caution with these prescriptions. Most of them have a cost for fencing, herbicide, and/or prescribed fire that may or may not be coupled with a first removal cut. If the costs are acceptable to the landowner, the prescriptions are recommended. Also, all prescriptions require a complete SILVAH inventory about 5 years after the treatments.

If the costs are unacceptable, we recommend no cutting as the interfering vegetation and/or browsing pressure by deer likely will result in a regeneration failure. In that case, the landowner needs to reevaluate his or her desire to increase the oak component of the regeneration pool, consider regenerating other desirable species, and consult prescriptions from Charts D or E.

**No Treatment, Reinventory**

This prescription is for stands with an adequate cohort of regeneration and no problems with deer, interfering vegetation, or dense understory shade. Such stands have more than 50-percent stocking of all oak or all established oak. There is little or no deer impact, less than 30-percent stocking of any interference, and less than 75-percent relative density. These stands need time for existing oak seedlings to grow to competitive size. It is best to not intervene at this time. Rather, do a complete SILVAH inventory in 5 to 10 years to determine the next treatment.

**Fence, Reinventory**

The stands requiring this prescription are nearly identical to those requiring a No Treatment, Reinventory prescription except that seedling stocking is adequate only if a fence is erected to exclude deer. Construct a fence per the instructions in the Fencing description. Wait for about 5 years and do a complete SILVAH inventory to determine the next treatment.

**Release Burn, Reinventory OR**
**Herbicide, Reinventory**

These two prescriptions are interchangeable depending on whether prescribed fire is an acceptable practice. They are intended for use in stands that contain at least 50 percent stocking of established oak and have no problems related to deer or overstory shade, but there is a problem with interfering vegetation. If prescribed fire is used, follow the instructions in the

Release Burn description. If herbicide is used, follow the instructions for one or more of the techniques in the Herbicide description. After applying these treatments, wait for about 5 years and do a complete SILVAH inventory to determine the next treatment.

### Fence, Release Burn, Reinventory OR
### Fence, Herbicide, Reinventory

These two prescriptions are interchangeable depending on whether prescribed fire is an acceptable practice. They are intended for use in stands that contain at least 50-percent stocking of established oak and overstory shade is not a problem, but deer and interfering vegetation do pose problems. If prescribed fire is used, follow the instructions in the Release Burn description. Construct a fence per the instructions in the Fencing description before the burn or immediately afterwards. If herbicide is used, follow the instructions for one or more of the techniques in the Herbicide description. It does not matter whether the fence is erected before or after the herbicide application so long as both occur within the same year. After applying these treatments, wait for about 5 years and do a complete SILVAH inventory to determine the next treatment.

### First Removal Cut, Reinventory

This prescription is appropriate for stands that are developing regeneration but lack sufficient light for the established oak seedlings to grow into the competitive size class. In such stands, at least 50 percent of the regeneration plots are stocked with established oak. There is minimal problem with interfering vegetation (stocking of 30-percent or less) and minimal impact from white-tailed deer (impact index less than 4). A harvest provides immediate income and no additional costs are incurred. Conduct the harvest per the instructions in the First Removal Cut description. In 5 to 10 years, do a complete SILVAH inventory of the stand to gauge the growth of the oak regeneration and determine whether any obstacles to regeneration have developed.

### Fence, First Removal Cut, Reinventory

This prescription is appropriate for stands with conditions that are nearly identical to those for the First Removal Cut, Reinventory prescription, except that a fence is needed to reduce deer browsing pressure. See the First Removal Cut and Fencing for detailed descriptions of these practices. Although the sequence of the fence installation and the timber harvest is not important, it probably is easier to erect the fence after the cutting. In 5 to 10 years, conduct a complete SILVAH inventory of the stand to gauge the growth of the oak regeneration and determine whether any obstacles to regeneration have developed.

### First Removal Cut, Release Burn, Reinventory OR
### First Removal Cut, Herbicide, Reinventory

There are two alternatives in this prescription. Both are applicable to stands with conditions similar to those requiring a First Removal Cut, Reinventory prescription, but are impacted by interfering vegetation. At least 30 percent of the plots are stocked with interfering vegetation or the basal area of undesirable saplings and poles exceeds 10 ft$^2$ per acre.

The first alternative, also known as the shelterwood and burn method (Brose and others 1999b), is applicable if burning the stand will be feasible in several years. To implement the shelterwood and burn method, conduct a partial harvest per the instructions in the First Removal Cut description. Be sure the logging slash does not accumulate at the bases of the valuable residual trees because the resultant intense fire will kill them (Fig.5.11). After the harvest, wait for the oak regeneration to develop its root systems **and** is overtopped by competing vegetation. This likely will occur within 3 to 5 years depending on site quality. Once the oak regeneration has reached competitive size and is overtopped by other species, conduct a prescribed burn per the instructions in the Release Burn description.

The second alternative substitutes herbicide for fire where burning is not feasible. The partial cut is the same as that for the fire alternative. After the cut, use one or more of the techniques in the Herbicide description to control interfering vegetation.

The understory light regime created by either alternative allows oak seedlings to develop into competitive stems in

Photos by Patrick Brose, Northern Research Station

Figure 5.11.—Prevent or remove slash accumulation at the base of valuable residual trees to protect them from an intense fire.

about 5 years while retarding the rapid height growth of other hardwood species. At that time, inventory the stand per SILVAH guidelines to determine the next treatment for the stand.

### Fence, First Removal Cut, Release Burn, Reinventory OR
### Fence, First Removal Cut, Herbicide, Reinventory

This prescription is appropriate for stands with conditions that are nearly identical to those described previously except that a fence is needed to exclude deer. Construct a fence per the instructions in the Fencing description. If prescribed fire will be used, the fence must be erected before or just after the first removal cut. Conduct a prescribed burn 3 to 5 years after the harvest per the guidelines in the Release Burn description. If applying herbicide, use one or more of the techniques in the Herbicide description. The sequence of treatments is not as important in the herbicide option as it is in the fire option. What is crucial is that they are applied within a year of each other. In about 5 years, conduct a complete SILVAH inventory to determine whether additional treatments are required.

## Chart H Prescriptions

Chart H recommends prescriptions to release established oak seedlings on medium- and low-quality sites where upland oak species typically are better competitors. All prescriptions on Chart H are the same as those prescribed on Chart F. See those descriptions for instructions. Three prescriptions on Chart H include only a final removal cut or a first removal cut if site limitations or the silvicultural system restrictions does not allow for a single complete harvest. They are highly recommended because they produce an income with little cost.

Depending on current conditions, three prescriptions recommend fencing to address problems posed by deer. We advise caution with these prescriptions because they require a cost. If the cost is acceptable to the landowner, the prescriptions are recommended.

If the cost is unacceptable, we recommend no cutting as the browsing pressure by deer likely will result in a regeneration failure. In that case, the landowner needs to reevaluate his or her desire to increase the oak component of the regeneration pool, consider regenerating other desirable species, and consult prescriptions from Charts D or E.

## Chart I Prescriptions

These prescriptions are intended for use in oak stands on all site types that are near the beginning of the regeneration process. Chart I prescriptions emphasize low-impact treatments aimed at developing new oak seedlings, the smallest of the three oak size classes, into established and competitive oaks. As a result, none of the Chart I prescriptions incorporates prescribed burning as fire readily kills new oaks.

We advise caution with these prescriptions because they require an initial investment (fencing and/or herbicide) with little or no income for 5 to 10 years. If the costs are acceptable to the landowner, the prescriptions are recommended. Also, a subsequent SILVAH inventory is required several years after implementation of the prescription.

If the costs are unacceptable, we recommend no cutting as the interfering vegetation and/or browsing pressure by deer likely will result in a regeneration failure. In that case, the landowner needs to reevaluate his or her desire to increase the oak component of the regeneration pool, consider regenerating other desirable species, and consult prescriptions from Charts D or E.

### No Treatment, Reinventory

See this prescription in the Chart G section. Wait 5 to 10 years before doing a SILVAH inventory to determine the next treatment.

### Fence, Reinventory

See this prescription in the Chart G section. Wait 5 to 10 years before doing a SILVAH inventory to determine the next treatment.

### Herbicide, Reinventory

See this prescription in the Chart G section. Wait 5 to 10 years before doing a SILVAH inventory to determine the next treatment.

### Fence, Herbicide, Reinventory

See this prescription in the Chart G section. Wait 5 to 10 years before doing a SILVAH inventory to determine the next treatment.

### Preparatory Cut, Reinventory

This prescription is appropriate for a stand that is in the process of developing regeneration but lacks sufficient light for new oak seedlings to grow into the established size class. Such stands have at least 50 percent of the regeneration plots stocked with all oak at ambient deer levels. Interfering vegetation has a minimal impact (present in less than 30 percent of the interference plots) and there is minimal impact from white-tailed deer (Deer Impact Index less than 4). A harvest provides limited income and no additional costs for other silvicultural treatments. Conduct a light partial harvest per the instructions in the Preparatory Cut description. In 5 to 10 years, do a complete SILVAH inventory of the stand to gauge the growth of the oak regeneration and to determine whether obstacles to regeneration have developed.

The preparatory cut may need to be a noncommercial treatment if a commercial harvest is not feasible due to local markets. In that case, use one or more of the **Herbicide** techniques to reduce the overstory from below to 70 percent relative density (Fig.5.12).

### Fence, Preparatory Cut, Reinventory

This prescription is appropriate for stands with conditions that are nearly identical to those for the Preparatory Cut, Reinventory prescription, except that the 50-percent all-oak stocking requirement is met only if a fence is erected to exclude deer. See the Preparatory Cut and Fencing descriptions for instructions. Erect the fence after the timber harvest. In 5 to 10 years, do a complete SILVAH inventory of the stand to gauge the growth of the oak regeneration and to determine whether obstacles to regeneration have developed.

Photo by Gary Miller, Northern Research Station

Figure 5.12.—A noncommercial preparatory cut can be accomplished with the individual stem herbicide techniques that remove the understory and midstory canopies that cast dense shade on the forest floor.

### Preparatory Cut, Herbicide, Reinventory

This prescription is appropriate for stands with conditions similar to those requiring a Preparatory Cut, Reinventory prescription except that interfering vegetation poses a problem (at least 30 percent of the plots are stocked with interfering vegetation or basal area of undesirable saplings and poles exceeds 10 ft$^2$ per acre).

Conduct a light partial cut according to the Preparatory Cut description. Then, apply one or more of the treatments described in the Herbicide description to control interfering vegetation. The understory light regime created by this prescription allows oak seedlings to develop into established stems in 5 to10 years while retarding the rapid height growth of other hardwood species. At that time, inventory the stand per SILVAH guidelines to determine the next treatment for the stand.

### Fence, Preparatory Cut, Herbicide, Reinventory

This prescription is appropriate for stands with conditions that are nearly identical to those for the Preparatory Cut, Herbicide, Reinventory prescription, except that a fence is needed to exclude deer. Conduct a light partial harvest per the Preparatory Cut description. Construct the fence per the instructions in the Fencing description. The preparatory cut will remove many non-oaks that likely will sprout so it may be prudent to erect the fence 2 or 3 years after the harvest so deer can browse the non-oak stump sprouts. Control interfering vegetation as appropriate with one or more of the techniques described in the Herbicide description. Timing of the herbicide application with the other treatments will depend on the type of interfering vegetation. Conduct a complete SILVAH inventory about 5 years after the last treatment to determine a future course of action.

## Chart J Prescriptions

Chart J prescriptions are for oak stands that are at the beginning of the oak regeneration process and are applicable on any site type. The objective is to establish natural oak regeneration from acorns when an adequate seed source is present. We cautiously recommend these prescriptions because they rely on the natural production of acorns—a sporadic event in the mid-Atlantic region—so a good to bumper acorn crop is essential (Fig.5.13).

Photo by Patrick Brose, Northern Research Station

Figure 5.13.—The oak regeneration process begins with an acorn crop of sufficient size that overcomes losses to disease, insects, wildlife, and weather and results in the formation of a new oak cohort.

We also advise caution with these prescriptions because most require an initial investment (fencing, herbicide, prescribed fire, and/or scarification) with little or no income for 5 to 10 years. If the costs are acceptable to the landowner, the prescriptions are cautiously recommended. Also, they require a subsequent stand inventory several years after the implementation of the prescription.

If the costs are unacceptable, we recommend no cutting as the interfering vegetation and/or browsing pressure by deer likely will result in a regeneration failure. In that case, the landowner needs to reevaluate his or her desire to increase the oak component of the regeneration pool, consider regenerating other desirable species, and consult prescriptions from Charts D or E.

### No Treatment, Monitor Acorns, Reinventory

This prescription is appropriate for stands that are between large acorn crops and not affected by deer, interfering vegetation, or shade. Such stands have an adequate seed source (at least 40 ft$^2$ of basal area/acre of oak species that are at least 12 inches d.b.h.) but are lacking oak regeneration (stocking of all oak is less than 50 percent). The Deer Impact Index is 3 or less, stocking of interfering vegetation is 30 percent or less, and stocking of thick duff also is 30 percent or less. These stands need time for an acorn crop to occur and for subsequent seedling establishment so it is best not to intervene at this time. Monitor acorn crops and inventory the stand 2 to 5 years after a good acorn crop has established a cohort of new oak seedlings to determine the next treatment.

### Fence, Monitor Acorns, Reinventory

Stands requiring this prescription are identical to those for No Treatment, Monitor Acorns, Reinventory except that a fence is required to exclude deer. Construct a fence per the instructions in the Fencing description. Monitor acorn crops and inventory the stand 2 to 5 years after a good acorn crop has established a cohort of new oak seedlings to determine the next treatment.

## Site Prep Burn, Monitor Acorns, Reinventory OR
## Herbicide, Monitor Acorns, Reinventory

These prescriptions are interchangeable and are appropriate for stands with conditions that are nearly identical to those described previously for No Treatment, Monitor Acorns, Reinventory except that interfering vegetation is a problem (more than 30-percent stocking or basal area of undesirable saplings and pole exceeds $10ft^2$/ac). If using fire, conduct one or more burns according to instructions in the Site Prep Burn description. If applying herbicide, use one or more of the methods described in the Herbicide description. Monitor acorn crops and inventory the stand 2 to 5 years after a good acorn crop has established a cohort of new oak seedlings to determine the next treatment.

## Fence, Site Prep Burn, Monitor Acorns, Reinventory OR
## Fence, Herbicide, Monitor Acorns, Reinventory

Either of these prescriptions is appropriate for stands with conditions similar to those for No Treatment, Monitor Acorns, Reinventory, except that a fence is needed to exclude deer and interfering vegetation is a problem ( more than 30 percent stocking or basal area of undesirable saplings and poles exceeds $10ft^2$/ac). Depending on the viability of burning the stand, conduct one or more prescribed fires or apply herbicides per the instructions in the Site Prep Burn or Herbicide descriptions. Construct a fence following the instructions in the Fencing description. It is important is that these treatments are applied within the same year. Monitor acorn crops and inventory the stand 2 to 5 years after a good acorn crop has established a cohort of new oak seedlings to determine the next treatment.

## Scarify, Monitor Acorns, Reinventory

This prescription is appropriate for stands similar to those described for No Treatment, Monitor Acorns, Reinventory except that there is a thick excessively thick duff layer (more than 2 inches) in at least 30 percent of the interference plots. Prepare the forest floor as a seedbed for acorns per the instructions in the Scarification description. Monitor acorn crops and inventory the stand 2 to 5 years after a good acorn crop has established a cohort of new oak seedlings to determine the next treatment.

## Fence, Scarify, Monitor Acorns, Reinventory

This prescription is appropriate for stands similar to those described for No Treatment, Monitor Acorns, Reinventory except that the Deer Impact Index is greater than 3 and there is a excessively thick duff layer (more than 2 inches) in at least 30 percent of the interference plots. Prepare the forest floor as a seedbed for acorns per the instructions in the Scarification description and construct a fence per instructions in the Fencing description. Monitor acorn crops and inventory the stand 2 to 5 years after a good acorn crop has established a cohort of new oak seedlings to determine the next treatment.

### Scarify, Herbicide, Monitor Acorns, Reinventory

This prescription is appropriate for stands similar to those described for No Treatment, Monitor Acorns, Reinventory except that there is interfering vegetation problem and a thick duff layer in at least 30 percent of the interference plots. Prepare the forest floor as a seedbed for acorns per the instructions in the Scarification description. If the interfering plants still pose a problem following scarification, apply an appropriate herbicide using one or more of the techniques described in the Herbicide description. Monitor acorn crops and inventory the stand 2 to 5 years after a good acorn crop has established a cohort of new oak seedlings to determine the next treatment.

### Fence, Scarify, Herbicide, Monitor Acorns, Reinventory

This prescription is appropriate for stands similar to those described for No Treatment, Monitor Acorns, Reinventory except that excessive deer browsing, interfering vegetation, and thick duff are obstacles. These stands are extremely difficult to regenerate and ignoring them while concentrating efforts on easier-to-regenerate stands may be the best approach. If they must be regenerated, prepare the forest floor as a seedbed for acorns per the instructions in the Scarification description. If the interfering plants still pose a problem following scarification, apply an appropriate herbicide using one or more of the techniques described in the Herbicide description. Finally, construct a fence per instructions in the Fencing description. Monitor acorn crops and inventory the stand 2 to 5 years after a good acorn crop has established a cohort of new oak seedlings to determine the next treatment.

## Chart K Prescriptions

Chart K prescriptions are intended for use in oak stands that have lost their seed source and in which are regeneration obstacles and little or no oak regeneration. These stands are extremely difficult to regenerate, require considerable investment, and offer no financial return in the foreseeable future. Our recommendation for such stands is that they not be treated and to allocate management resources to stands with a higher regeneration potential, or that they be allowed to convert to another forest type or plant community.

If the landowner wishes to regenerate such oak stands, we offer these artificial-regeneration prescriptions as considerations rather than as recommendations. Johnson and others (2002) and Dey and others (2008) provide thorough discussions on the intricacies associated with planting oaks. Major considerations are:

1) Obtain high-quality oak seedlings from a reputable nursery for planting. The number needed will depend on the management objectives but 50 to 200 oak seedlings per acre is not uncommon.

2) High-quality oak planting stock will have a basal diameter of about 3/8 inch with the roots pruned to equal lengths and the stem cut back to about 8 inches in height.

3) Plant the seedlings in the spring and be sure the planting hole is large enough and deep enough to accommodate the roots.

4) Select suitable planting sites so that seedlings will receive adequate sunlight and there is minimal competition from other plants. If the overstory is producing some shade (more than 20-percent relative density or approximate 20 ft$^2$ of basal area/acre), perform a

Liberation Cut per the instructions in the description of this practice. This is especially important if tree shelters are being used to protect the oak seedlings (Schuler and others 2005).

5) If deer browsing poses a problem, it may be less expensive to install and maintain plastic tree shelters or wire cages than to construct area wide fencing.

6) If interfering vegetation poses a problem and fire is the preferred control method, do a Site Prep Burn before the seedlings are planted. If herbicides are used, use one or more of the techniques described in the Herbicide description.

7) Once oaks are planted, they have the same needs and problems as naturally-regenerated oaks so the previous prescriptions are appropriate depending on deer browse pressure, competing vegetation, and site quality.

# CHAPTER 6: POSTHARVEST FOLLOW-UP AND CROP-TREE MANAGEMENT

**Patrick Brose, Gary Miller, and Todd Ristau**

An integral part of all the final removal cut prescriptions is a postharvest follow-up examination of the oak regeneration. Evaluating the adequacy of oak reproduction is as important after the final harvest as it was prior to harvest because competitive-size oak stems have a survival rate to age 20 of 10 to 50 percent, depending on site quality, interspecies competitive relationships, and stochastic events (Loftis 1990a, Sander and others 1976). For example, interference may develop should pin cherry (*Prunus pensylvanica*) seeds stored in the forest floor germinate en masse or should wind-blown black birch seeds invade the stand (Fig. 6.1). These species pose a serious threat to oak and other desirable hardwood regeneration in the early years of stand development (Ristau and Horsley 1999, 2006). Similarly, excessive deer browsing may occur depending on size of the local herd, hunting pressure, winter weather, and the availability of other food sources in the vicinity of the stand.

Photos by Patrick Brose, Northern Research Station

Figure 6.1.—Interference can develop after the final removal cut when seeds stored in the forest floor germinate or are carried in by the wind.

The initial follow-up evaluation occurs about 5 years after the final harvest. Ideally, this is done in the early spring or winter months when it is easiest to move through the young stand (Fig. 6.2). Use 6-foot-radius plots at a density of one plot per acre and locate them to uniformly cover the stand. If the management goal is an Allegheny or northern hardwood stand with no emphasis on culturing oak (it is one of several desirable species), then record the number of stems by species and size class as per the Allegheny and Northern Hardwood Postharvest Follow-up Tally Sheet (Appendix 4) and use the Chart L decision chart. If the management goal is to create an oak-dominated stand, use the Mixed-Oak Postharvest Follow-up Tally Sheet (Appendix 5) and the Chart M decision chart. Note that neither chart is programmed into the SILVAH system at this time so you must calculate the variables and navigate the charts by hand. The oak prescription may recommend one or more of the practices described in Chapter 5 to correct a problem.

Managing an oak stand with the SILVAH system usually results in a Chart M prescription of **Commence Crop Tree Management in 10 Years**. Generally, crop-tree release (CTR) is considered an intermediate treatment (Miller and others 2007) but we have included it here because it is a transitional practice between the regeneration and intermediate stand management phases and can ensure the long-term survival of the oak stems and profoundly shape species composition of the new stand.

Photo by Patrick Brose, Northern Research Station

Figure 6.2.—Postharvest stands are inventoried 3 to 5 years after the final cut and are easiest in the winter or early spring.

Oak reproduction should be evaluated for CTR about 10 to 20 years after the final harvest depending on site quality. In even-aged stand development, this is when the dominant and codominant trees begin to form a closed canopy. Although the young stand still contains thousands of trees per acre, only those in the upper crown classes likely will remain competitive for many years. Also, trees that attain dominant and codominant status at canopy closure respond well to CTR with respect to faster d.b.h. growth and crown-class retention. Such a reliable response among upper canopy trees provides the forest manager with an opportunity to sustain individual oak trees for many years, which, in turn, provides a means of reaching oak stocking goals as the stand matures.

Four factors require close attention when determining whether CTR is needed in young oak stands to achieve long-term oak stocking goals:

1) A *realistic oak* stocking goal must be specified with respect to the percentage of oak relative density at maturity and the number of overstory oaks needed to achieve that composition.

2) The *characteristics of desirable oak crop trees* in young stands must be defined so that an appropriate analysis of treatment needs can be conducted.

3) An *inventory of oak crop trees* is needed to estimate the abundance and competitive status in the new stand being evaluated.

4) An *estimate of oak crop tree survival* is needed to determine whether follow-up CTR treatments are needed to attain oak stocking goals.

The remainder of this chapter provides information on the effect of CTR treatments in young oak stands. In some stands where oak crop trees are abundant and well distributed, such treatments may not be justified. In other stands where the availability of oak crop trees is more limited, CTR treatments may be crucial for maintaining desired species composition in the future. Additional information is provided on proper timing and application methods for conducting CTR treatments.

# Realistic Stocking Goal for Oak

Prescribing silvicultural treatments in young oak stands requires that the long-term goals for species composition in the mature stand be well defined. A goal for species composition can be stated in general terms, e.g., percentage of total basal area or percentage of total relative density. For example, the forest manager may desire a stand in which oaks occupy 50 percent of relative density at maturity. When evaluating young stands, it is helpful to state oak stocking goals in more specific terms, e.g., the number of overstory oaks per acre needed at maturity. Species composition in pole and sawtimber stands is relatively stable but natural competition in young sapling stands can lead to unexpected changes in species composition over several decades. Young stands contain thousands of trees per acre, so it can be difficult to assess how changes in crown class and the competitiveness of individual trees might affect species composition as the stand develops. Setting a specific "number of trees" goal allows the forest manager to focus attention on a relatively small number of trees in the young stand to determine whether follow-up silvicultural treatments are needed to enhance the development of preferred species.

Empirical data for setting realistic oak stocking goals were obtained from 54 mature oak stands in Pennsylvania, West Virginia, Ohio, and Kentucky (Table 6.1). The stands ranged in age from 54 to 110 years and had no history of major disturbances for several decades before data were collected. Site index base age 50 for northern red oak ranged from 60 to 86. Oaks accounted for an average of 65 percent of total basal area with most of the oak stocking in the upper crown classes. The remaining basal area included a small number of non-oaks in the upper canopy and mostly shade-tolerant species in the suppressed understory. In general, stand stocking and structure conditions were typical of oak-dominated stands in which the SILVAH-OAK decision-support system is intended to be applied.

Average stand structure conditions indicated that the overstory of mature oak stands contained 58 trees/acre in the dominant and codominant crown classes and 49 trees/acre in the intermediate crown class (Table 6.1). The number of oaks in the upper canopy (dominant and codominant trees) averaged 41 trees/acre. The number of intermediate oaks averaged 25 trees/acre. Suppressed trees accounted for a negligible proportion of stand stocking, and nearly all of them were non-oak species. The data indicated that a goal of 65-percent oak basal area was achieved with an average of 41 upper canopy oaks/acre plus 25 intermediate oaks/acre at stand maturity.

Table 6.1.—Average species composition and structure of 54 mature oak stands[a] in Pennsylvania, West Virginia, Ohio, and Kentucky (standard error in parentheses)

| Species | Crown class | | | | | Basal area ft²/ac |
|---|---|---|---|---|---|---|
| | Dominant | Co-dominant | Intermediate | Suppressed | Total | |
| | ----------------------------------------------trees/acre---------------------------------------------- | | | | | |
| Oaks | 3 (0.4) | 38 (2.0) | 25 (3.4) | 16 (2.8) | 82 (6.8) | 75 (2.5) |
| Others | 1 (0.2) | 16 (2.0) | 24 (2.4) | 122 (15.3) | 164 (14.9) | 40 (3.0) |
| Total | 4 (0.6) | 54 (2.4) | 49 (4.2) | 138 (16.6) | 245 (18.4) | 115 (2.7) |

[a]Stand age ranges from 54 to 110 years, site index base age 50 ranges from 60 to 86, and stand area ranges from 6 to 46 acres.

Similar goals for number of overstory oaks can be derived from published stocking equations developed for upland oak and mixed-species stands (Gingrich 1967, Stout and Nyland 1986). For example, individual oaks that are 18 inches d.b.h. account for about 1.3 percent of relative stand density. To achieve 50-percent oak relative density the mature stand must contain at least 39 oaks/acre of that average size, and they would most likely occupy dominant or codominant crown classes (Table 6.2). At any stocking level, the stand probably would contain some additional oaks in the intermediate class that would contribute to oak stocking and serve as insurance in achieving the desired species composition.

**Table 6.2.—Number of overstory oaks per acre needed at stand maturity to achieve oak stocking goals**

| Oak stocking goal at stand maturity (% oak relative density) | Minimum number of overstory oaks needed[a] (trees/acre) |
|---|---|
| 20 | 15 |
| 30 | 23 |
| 40 | 31 |
| 50 | 39 |
| 60 | 46 |
| 70 | 54 |
| 80 | 62 |

[a] Includes dominant and codominant oaks, 18 inches or larger d.b.h. and each overstory oak represents a relative density of 1.3 percent or greater (Stout and Nyland 1986).

Goals for oak stocking vary according to long-term management objectives, and cultural treatments in young stands often can help attain them. **A good rule of thumb is to promote approximately one oak crop tree in the young stand for every percentage point of oak stocking desired in the mature stand.** For example, a goal of 50-percent oak stocking can be attained by seeking to sustain about 50 oak crop trees when the stand is young. Not all young oak crop trees can be sustained in the overstory for several decades but using such a guide in young stands allows for the loss of several trees and provides a reasonable margin for error in reaching stocking goals.

## Characteristics of Oak Crop Trees

An oak crop tree is one that exhibits desirable characteristics that help meet management objectives, can respond to CTR, and can remain competitive for many years. Management objectives vary among landowners, often focusing on wildlife habitat, maintaining stand diversity, producing timber, or forest health. For each landowner or individual stand, the criteria used to define a crop tree also can differ. However, in all cases, crop trees must have a crown structure and canopy position that allow them to respond to release and remain competitive as the stand matures. Crop trees are found almost exclusively in the dominant and codominant crown classes. In limited cases, oaks in strong intermediate classes can be released if this practice is critical for meeting management objectives. However, in most cases, trees in the suppressed or intermediate classes will not respond acceptably to CTR. Crop trees can be selected to meet multiple objectives in the same stand and selection criteria often can be adjusted to accommodate unique circumstances.

The purpose of CTR is to reduce competition around selected trees so that they improve in vigor, remain competitive in the stand, and provide desired future benefits. Note that the purpose of CTR comprises several key concepts that guide the forest manager in selecting appropriate crop trees. Key characteristics to consider in selecting crop trees are species, crown class, origin, bole quality, vigor, and risk. It is important to select trees that are adapted to local site conditions.

**Species.** This is the primary factor that defines a crop tree's capacity to meet management objectives. Market value, wildlife value, and more subtle benefits such as aesthetics, diversity, and recreation are determined by the species composition in the stand. Once management objectives are defined, candidate species for crop trees will become clear. Crop trees usually have a relatively high value in local markets and provide suitable seed production for future regeneration and food for wildlife. Crop trees diversify the species mix in the overstory which provides a range of other benefits and reduce the risk of insect and disease attacks associated with low species diversity. Some species can be relatively scarce or only several representatives may remain within a stand. If site conditions are suitable, including such trees in the CTR prescription helps ensure species diversity.

**Crown Class.** Crop trees must be able to compete successfully after release in the forest community and live long enough to provide benefits that meet management objectives. Thus, crop trees usually are found in dominant or codominant crown classes. For shade-intolerant and midtolerant species, the survival rate for crop trees in the dominant or codominant classes usually exceeds 90 percent for decades after CTR. Trees in intermediate or suppressed classes, particularly shade-intolerant species, generally do not respond well to CTR. Height growth for these trees usually is too slow to keep pace with codominant competitors. Similarly, several subordinate trees of midtolerant species such as the oaks can be enhanced by CTR to grow into the upper crown classes, though the success rate in improving crown class usually is less than 20 percent. Trees in the intermediate class should be selected only as a last resort, and the forest manager should expect limited long-term success following the investment.

**Origin.** Trees of seedling- and sprout-origin can be acceptable crop trees. Sprout-origin crop trees should exhibit low attachment to the parent stump and, if possible, be located on the uphill side of the stump. Some sprout clumps have more than one acceptable crop tree in the same clump. In such cases, select the two best trees, preferably with a U-shape connection between them, and release around both crowns as if they are one.

**Bole Quality, Vigor, and Risk.** Crop-tree quality, vigor, and risk are closely related. Several research trials indicated that young hardwood trees with straight, defect-free boles tend to retain these qualities as they grow (Miller and Stringer 2004, Miller et al. 2007, Sonderman 1986). In addition, early CTR in young stands has little adverse effect on bole quality (Miller 2000). Desirable crop trees have straight boles, no forks in the bottom 17-foot bole section, no evidence of disease or damage, and smooth bark with a healthy, normal appearance. Evidence of epicormic branching before release indicates that the tree is already under stress and is likely to form more branches after release. Crop trees also have healthy crowns with a live crown ratio of at least 30 percent and no evidence of crown dieback.

**Site Quality.** Hardwood species exhibit varying degrees of competitiveness depending on site quality. For example, yellow-poplar is extremely competitive and long lived on moist cove sites with deep soil, but grows slowly and is short lived on dry ridge sites with shallow soil. Select crop trees that are well adapted to site conditions to minimize the risk of poor performance or even mortality over several decades. Consider how individual trees can compete within a given plant community through periods of drought or other adverse conditions. Annual precipitation and elevation can act as environmental filters such that only certain species remain competitive for long periods above or below certain thresholds (Oliver and Larson 1996). Among hardwood species, soil texture, nutrient content, average annual precipitation, and even wind can affect competitiveness and longevity. Draw on local experience and professional judgment to select crop trees that can compete well and reach the desired age on the site.

## Inventory of Oak Crop Trees

Culturing oak crop trees in young stands requires an investment of time and money, so it is important to apply such treatments only in stands where the potential benefits exceed the costs. Improving the proportion of high-value species and high-quality trees in the overstory is the primary justification for applying CTR in young hardwood stands. Other benefits include faster d.b.h. growth and perhaps improved stand quality. Potential benefits are best in stands where high-value crop trees (due to species or quality) are threatened by aggressive, low-value competitors. The process of recognizing candidate stands for CTR or prioritizing treatments among multiple stands begins with a relatively simple inventory of the crop trees.

Collect data on crop trees and the competitors within each stand. Small, fixed-area circular plots are preferred in young hardwood stands, but any reliable sampling system is acceptable. Generally, 12-foot-radius (0.01 acre) plots are used at a density of one plot per acre for stands 10 to 15 years old. Older stands (age 15 to 20 years) and stands with high variability may require more plots or larger plots (16.7-foot radius or 0.02 acre). The important thing to remember is the plot size needs to capture the structure of the overstory trees and account for variability within the stand.

Within each plot, record the species and competitive status code for each crop tree based on its crown class and the relative aggressiveness of its adjacent competitors (Appendix 6). This step requires an understanding of site quality and how it affects competitive interactions among species. The purpose of this step is to assess the likely effect of CTR on each crop tree's long-term ability to compete. Later, this information will be aggregated for all crop trees in the stand to determine the likely impact of CTR on future species composition. A brief definition of each competitive status code follows.

### Competitive Status Codes

1) Dominant or strong codominant crop trees that are likely to survive without release. These trees, often of vigorous seedling-or sprout-origin, are expected to compete well without CTR.

2) Codominant crop trees that are not immediately threatened by adjacent trees. These crop trees are flanked by trees of the same height and crown size. They might become threatened if neighboring trees become more aggressive. These crop trees will become strong codominants if released.

3) Weak codominant crop trees that are threatened by adjacent trees and are unlikely to remain competitive in the main canopy without release. Neighboring trees usually are larger, fast-growing trees or aggressive sprout clumps. These crop trees can remain codominant if released in the near future.

4) Desirable crop trees in the intermediate crown class. Crown vigor indicates that such trees remain capable of responding to release but CTR is needed immediately to prevent further decline. Examples include shade-tolerant maples or midtolerant oaks. The proportion of trees in this competitive status that can become codominant following CTR depends on initial vigor and height differential when released.

**Table 6.3.—Example of predicting the number of overstory oaks at stand maturity (oak crop trees in dominant or codominant crown classes) based on inventory of oak crop trees by initial competitive status from a 16-year-old stand with and without crop-tree release (CTR)**

| Competitive status | Inventory | With CTR treatment | | Without CTR treatment | |
|---|---|---|---|---|---|
| | | Probability | Predicted number | Probability | Predicted number |
| | No./acre | % | No./acre | % | No./acre |
| 1 | 10 | 95 | 9.5 | 75 | 7.5 |
| 2 | 20 | 90 | 18.0 | 50 | 10.0 |
| 3 | 20 | 75 | 15.0 | 25 | 5.0 |
| 4 | 30 | 20 | 6.0 | 5 | 1.5 |
| Totals | 80 | | 48.5 | | 24.0 |

Record the species and origin of competing trees within each plot but be careful not to double-count competitors whose crowns compete with more than one crop tree. Competing trees are adjacent to the crop trees, their crowns touch that of the crop tree, and they usually are dominant or codominant. The purpose of this step is to determine which species is the most likely to replace crop trees if they are unable to remain competitive in the overstory. Information on the species and origin of competing trees is useful in planning herbicide or mechanical release methods. Note that plots with no crop trees also have no competitors to record.

## Predicting the Number of Overstory Oaks at Maturity

The first step in analyzing the inventory data is to tabulate the number of crop trees per acre according to their competitive status (Table 6.3, Appendix 7). For example, the data in Table 6.3 is from an inventory of a 16-year-old hardwood stand with an oak site index of 70. The stand contained 80 crop trees per acre from the four competitive status groups. As a result, not all of them are expected to remain competitive in the overstory as the stand matures. In fact, many will perish from natural competition. Follow-up treatments such as CTR can be applied to increase the competitiveness and probability of long-term survival. Note that the probability of survival decreases as competitive status declines, but increases when CTR is applied. For example, about 75 percent of crop trees with competitive status 1 are expected to survive without CTR and about 95 percent are expected to survive with CTR. Appropriate survival rates are applied to the number of trees by competitive status and the results are summed. While the stand contained 80 crop trees per acre based on the inventory, only 24 crop trees per acre are expected to persist in the upper canopy without CTR, and 48 crop trees per acre are expected to persist in the upper canopy with CTR (Table 6.3, bottom row).

There is relatively little information available on estimating how CTR affects the probability that a tree will persist in the overstory. The probabilities presented in Table 6.3 are general estimates obtained from several sites in the upland hardwood region (Lamson and Smith 1978, Miller 2000, Mitchell et al. 1988, Schlesinger 1978, Schuler 2006, Ward 1995, Ward and Stephens 1994, Wendel and Lamson 1987). The probabilities can be adjusted based on local conditions and professional judgment.

# Decision Criteria for Prescribing Follow-up CTR Treatments

Key concepts and decision criteria for prescribing CTR treatment in young stands are summarized here and presented in Decision Chart N. The decision criteria were derived from the average number of overstory oaks per acre found in mature oak stands and observed long-term survival rates of oak crop trees in young stands. This approach requires the forest manager to set a realistic goal for oak stocking in the mature stand and to obtain an inventory of oak crop trees in the young stand being evaluated.

Goals for oak stocking must be expressed in the target number of overstory oaks needed at stand maturity. For example, the overstory of mature oak stands contain from 50 to 60 dominant and codominant trees per acre, including both oaks and competing species. In stands with relatively high oak stocking (oak relative density of 60 percent or more), oaks account for 40 to 45 of the overstory trees/acre plus 20 to 25 of intermediate trees/acre at maturity (Table 6.1). With a long-term goal in mind, the forest manager then determines whether silvicultural treatments are needed to enhance the competitiveness and survival of oak crop trees in the young stand.

The number of young oak crop trees expected to occupy a dominant or codominant position at stand maturity can be determined using the probabilities provided in Appendix 7. Probability estimates are provided for both untreated stands and those in which CTR is applied at an early age. Note that the probabilities are greater in stands where CTR treatments are applied. However, even under ideal conditions, not all dominant and codominant oaks in young hardwood sapling stands will persist in the overstory until stand maturity.

To determine whether CTR treatments are needed, collect crop-tree inventory data (Appendix 6), summarize it, enter it into the crop tree calculation sheet (Appendix 7) and multiply by the probabilities to determine the predicted number of overstory oaks for both untreated and treated stands. Compare the predicted number of overstory oaks for treated and untreated stands to the minimum number needed at stand maturity to achieve your stocking goal (Table 6.2). For example, if the predicted number of overstory oaks in untreated stands is at least 39 trees/acre, the CTR treatment is not needed to achieve 50-percent oak stocking. However, if the predicted number of overstory oaks in untreated stands falls short of 39 trees/acre, CTR is recommended to enhance the vigor and competitiveness of the available oak crop trees in the young stand.

In some cases, it may not be possible to reach 50-percent oak stocking at maturity—even with CTR treatments—because there are insufficient oak crop trees in the young stand. Still, CTR may be needed to retain as much oak stocking as possible to partially meet other goals related to species composition. CTR treatment costs usually are justified if the treated stand will contain at least 10 additional overstory oaks/acre compared to the untreated stand. Oaks usually have higher market values than the competitors, so increasing the number of overstory oaks at maturity increases the stand value and offsets the cost of earlier CTR treatments.

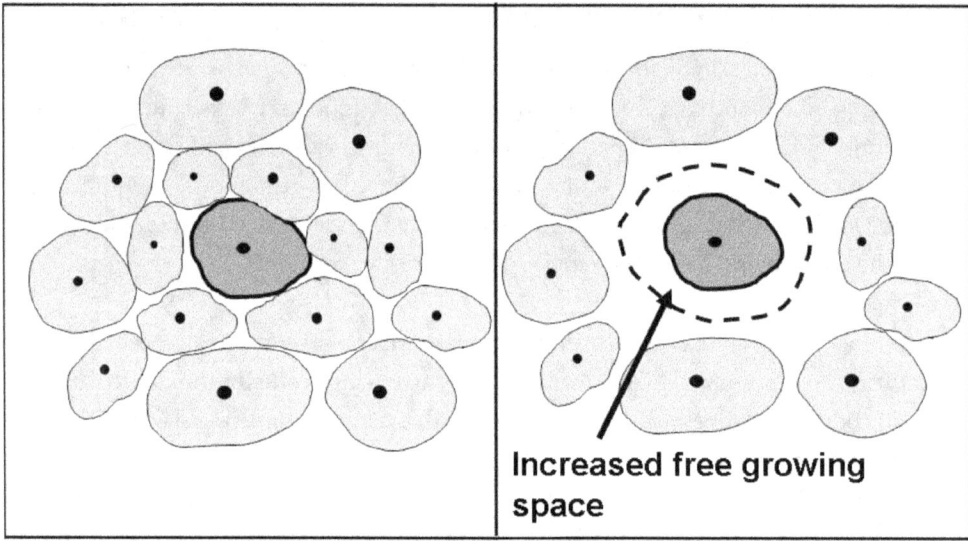

**Increased free growing space**

Figure 6.3.—A crop-tree crown (green) is shown from above the forest canopy. The diagram at left represents a crop-tree crown before release with six adjacent competitors. The diagram at right shows the free growing space available when a crown-touching release is applied to remove competing trees from all sides of a crop tree.

## Applying Crown-Touching Release

CTR is applied by increasing the growing space around the crowns of desirable trees (Lamson et al. 1990; Miller et al. 2007). This entails eliminating trees that are limiting the horizontal crown expansion of the crop tree, thus increasing its free growing space. A crown-touching release is applied to deaden or fell adjacent competing trees whose crowns touch that of the crop tree (Fig 6.3). The increase in growing space provides more sunlight and belowground resources to the crop tree. The crop tree can then develop more leaf area in its crown, increasing photosynthesis and growth. Improved vigor and crown size also has the potential to improve the seed production of individual trees (Healy et al. 1999, Johnson et al. 2002).

CTR can be used to provide various degrees of release based on the proportion of the crown that is left free to grow (Fig. 6.4). It is not necessary to remove or deaden adjacent trees whose crowns are beneath the crop tree because they are not interfering significantly with the crown of the crop tree (Fig. 6.5). In most cases, it is beneficial to retain trees in the overtopped and weak intermediate classes adjacent to crop trees. Such trees might be important for wildlife and aesthetics and they can protect timber quality and value by shading the crop-tree bole and reducing exposure to sunlight that can trigger epicormic branching. The key to effective CTR is focusing on identifying the desirable trees to favor rather than the undesirable trees to eliminate.

Providing more than a crown-touching release in young stands can have an adverse effect on future merchantable log height and stem quality. Too much free growing space retards total height growth until the canopy gaps close and allows more time for epicormic branches to form and reduce the development of clear stem (Miller 2000). Providing too much release also increases the risk of damage from wind, ice, and wet snow because the crop tree has little support from its distant neighbors. A simple crown-touching release is a good tradeoff between free growing space to enhance crop tree growth and quick canopy closure to maintain height growth and clear-stem development.

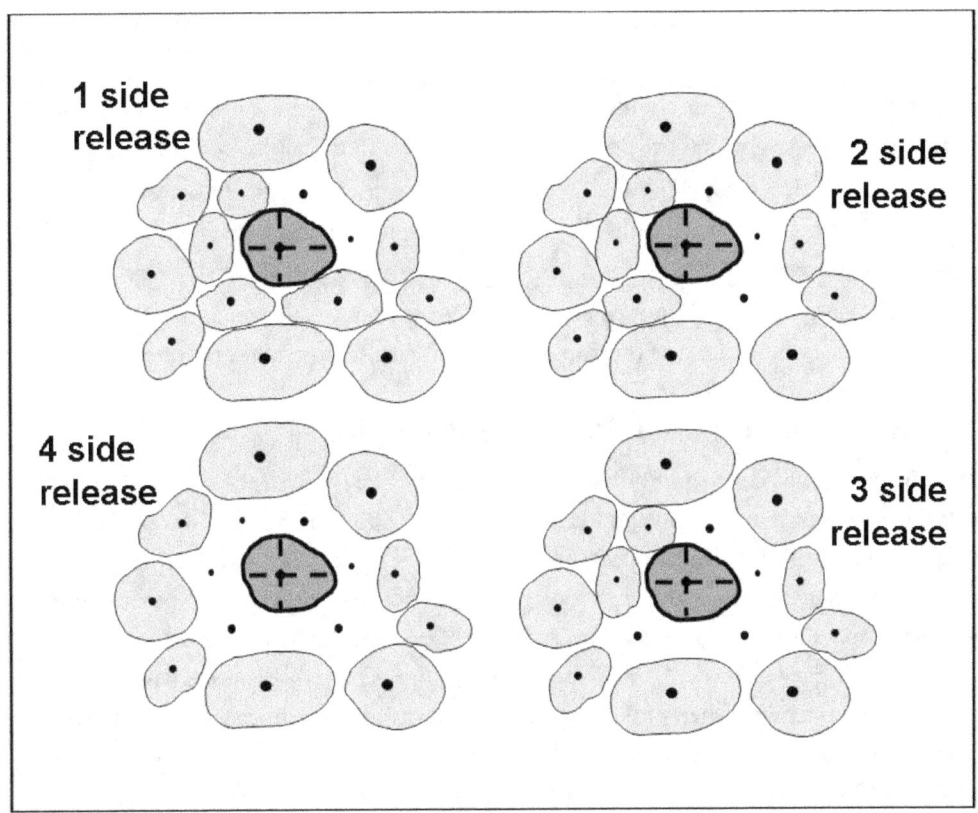

Figure 6.4.—A crop tree crown (green) is shown from above the forest canopy. The diagram shows a partial and full crown-touching release where one, two, three, or all four sides of the crop trees are released.

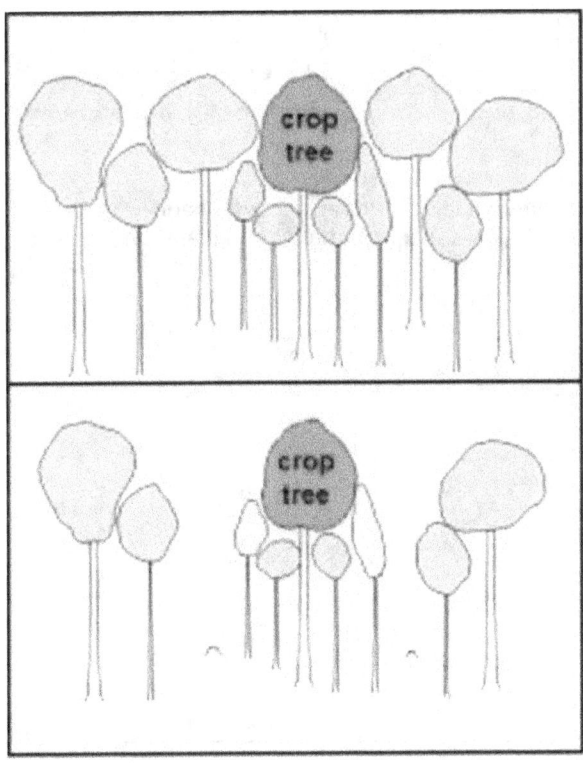

Figure 6.5.—Subordinate trees in overtopped or weak intermediate crown classes need not be removed to release crop trees.

69

Based on research and practical operational concerns, the following guidelines for the crown-touching release will help improve the effectiveness of CTR treatments.

1) Full crown-touching release should be considered for rapidly growing species such as some oaks, black cherry, yellow-poplar, and young trees in the sapling or pole stage.

2) Less than a full crown-touching release (at least three sides released) can be used for small sawtimber crop trees to limit the risk of epicormic branching where timber quality is a concern.

3) Subcanopy trees should be retained around crop trees to protect them and add other benefits to the stand so long as they do not conflict with management objectives.

## Why Focus Attention on a Few Overstory Trees?

Mature hardwood stands contain hundreds of trees per acre but those in the overstory account for the vast majority of stand volume and value. Data from a 53-year-old hardwood stand in the central Appalachians illustrate this important characteristic (Table 6.4). This stand regenerated naturally after clearcutting for charcoal in the 1930s with no interim silvicultural treatments or other disturbances. All trees 1 inch or larger in d.b.h. in twenty 0.5-acre permanent plots were tallied and assigned a stumpage value by species and merchantable volume based on local market prices. The trees were then ranked in order of increasing value in each plot and the average per-acre results were computed for all 20 plots. Cumulative totals for basal area, board foot volume, and stumpage value were tabulated for the 70 most valuable trees per acre (Table 6.4). For example, the 10 most valuable trees per acre accounted for 15 percent of stand basal area, 32 percent of stand volume, and 45 percent of stand value. The 20 most valuable trees per acre accounted for 63 percent of stand value and so on. In addition, the overstory included 69 trees per acre in the dominant or codominant crown classes and all of them were represented in the 70 most valuable trees/acre.

A closer examination of these data also indicated the importance of overstory species composition in determining stand value. For example, 56 percent of the stand value was in only 20 overstory trees/acre (8 black cherry and 12 northern red oak) (Fig. 6.6). The overstory

Table 6.4.—Cumulative basal-area stocking, merchantable volume, and stumpage value for the 70 most valuable trees/acre in a 53-year-old upland hardwood stand on site index 70

| Ascending tree value ranking (Trees/acre) | Stocking | Volume[a] | Stumpage value |
|---|---|---|---|
| | % of total | | |
| 10 | 15 | 32 | 45 |
| 20 | 26 | 53 | 63 |
| 30 | 34 | 69 | 76 |
| 40 | 41 | 80 | 93 |
| 50 | 48 | 89 | 93 |
| **60 trees** | **53%** | **95%** | **98%** |
| 70 | 58 | 99 | 99 |
| Total   441 | 143 ft²/ac | 13.7 MBF/acre | $3,925/acre |

[a]International ¼-inch rule.

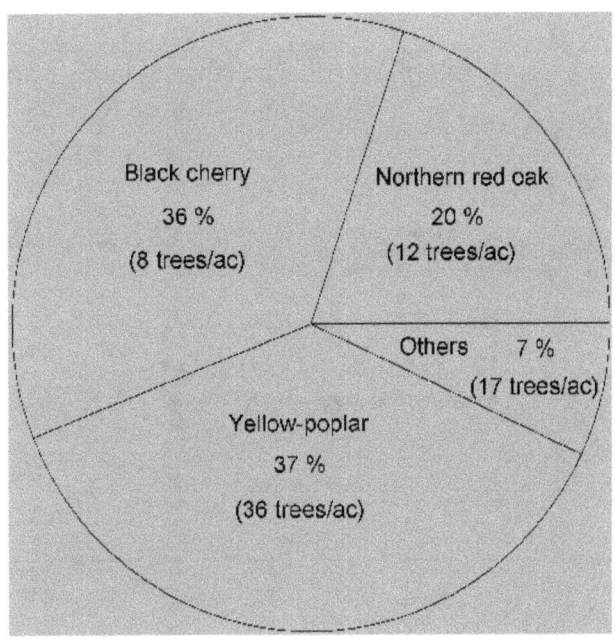

Figure 6.6.—Distribution of stand value by species and number of merchantable trees per acre in each species group.

had nearly twice as many yellow-poplar (36 trees/acre) that accounted for 37 percent of the stand value. Stand value was determined solely by natural competition for more than 50 years. The application of CTR treatments when the stand was still young (age 10 to 20 years), would have increased the proportion of black cherry and red oak that survived in the overstory, thus increasing stand value at maturity.

This example illustrates that nearly all of the economic value in hardwood stands is in a relatively small number of trees per acre. Forest managers need to focus on favoring all of the available crop trees, up to about 60 to 70 trees/acre. This upper threshold is determined by d.b.h./crown-diameter relationships for each species (Lamson 1987, Miller et al. 2006). In rare cases, in which there are more than 60 to 70 crop trees/acre, these trees can be released when the stand is still young and some can be removed later during a commercial thinning. Hardwood stands usually contain less than the 60 to 70 crop trees/acre recommended here, so most CTR prescriptions entail releasing a smaller (manageable) number of crop trees per acre.

Chart L
Allegheny and Northern Hardwoods
Postharvest Follow-up

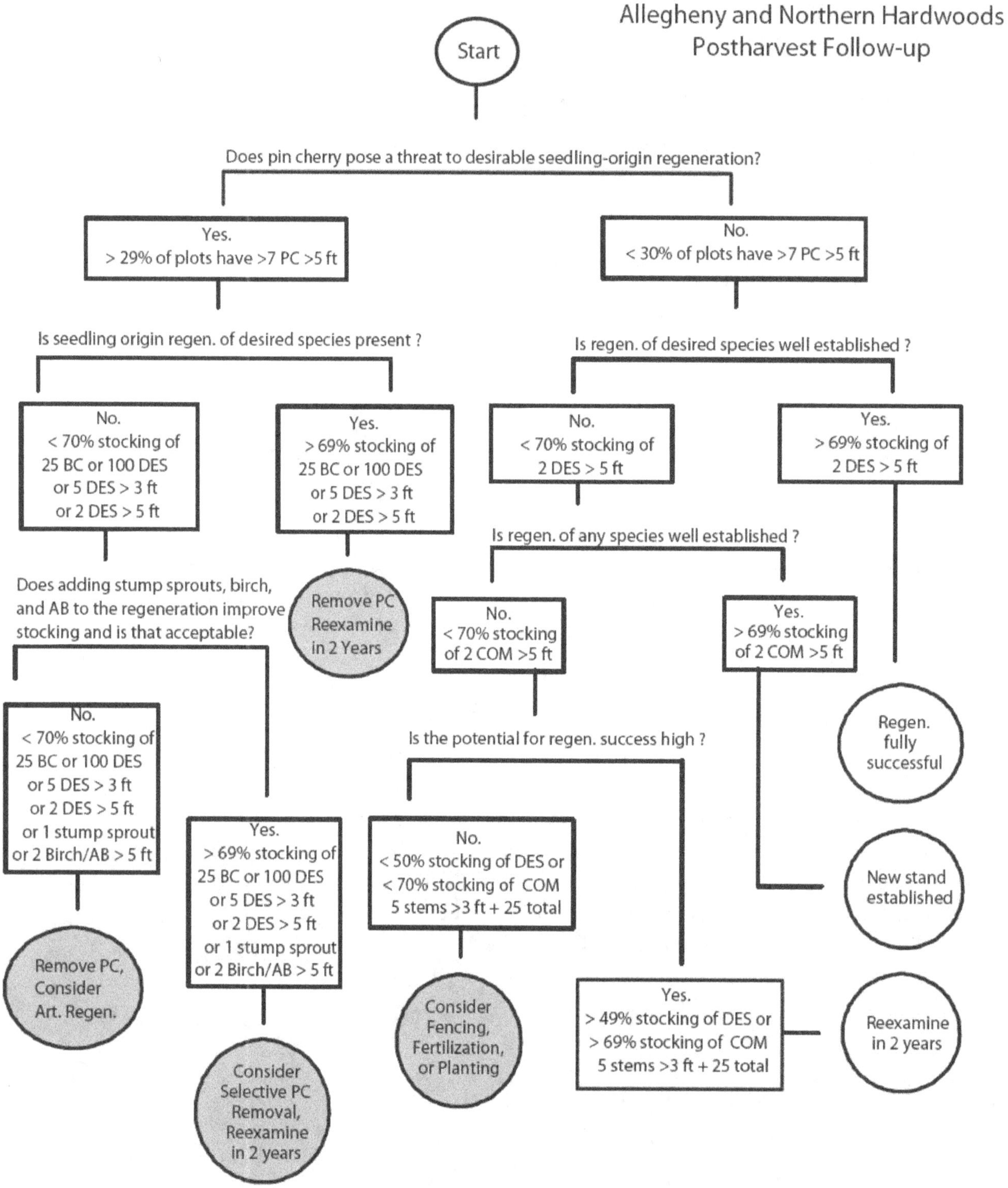

Start

Does pin cherry pose a threat to desirable seedling-origin regeneration?

**Yes.**
> 29% of plots have >7 PC >5 ft

**No.**
< 30% of plots have >7 PC >5 ft

Is seedling origin regen. of desired species present ?

**No.**
< 70% stocking of
25 BC or 100 DES
or 5 DES > 3 ft
or 2 DES > 5 ft

**Yes.**
> 69% stocking of
25 BC or 100 DES
or 5 DES > 3 ft
or 2 DES > 5 ft

Is regen. of desired species well established ?

**No.**
< 70% stocking of
2 DES > 5 ft

**Yes.**
> 69% stocking of
2 DES > 5 ft

Does adding stump sprouts, birch,
and AB to the regeneration improve
stocking and is that acceptable?

Remove PC
Reexamine
in 2 Years

Is regen. of any species well established ?

**No.**
< 70% stocking
of 2 COM >5 ft

**Yes.**
> 69% stocking
of 2 COM >5 ft

**No.**
< 70% stocking of
25 BC or 100 DES
or 5 DES > 3 ft
or 2 DES > 5 ft
or 1 stump sprout
or 2 Birch/AB > 5 ft

**Yes.**
> 69% stocking of
25 BC or 100 DES
or 5 DES > 3 ft
or 2 DES > 5 ft
or 1 stump sprout
or 2 Birch/AB > 5 ft

Is the potential for regen. success high ?

Regen.
fully
successful

**No.**
< 50% stocking of DES or
< 70% stocking of COM
5 stems >3 ft + 25 total

New stand
established

Remove PC,
Consider
Art. Regen.

Consider
Fencing,
Fertilization,
or Planting

**Yes.**
> 49% stocking of DES or
> 69% stocking of COM
5 stems >3 ft + 25 total

Reexamine
in 2 years

Consider
Selective PC
Removal,
Reexamine
in 2 years

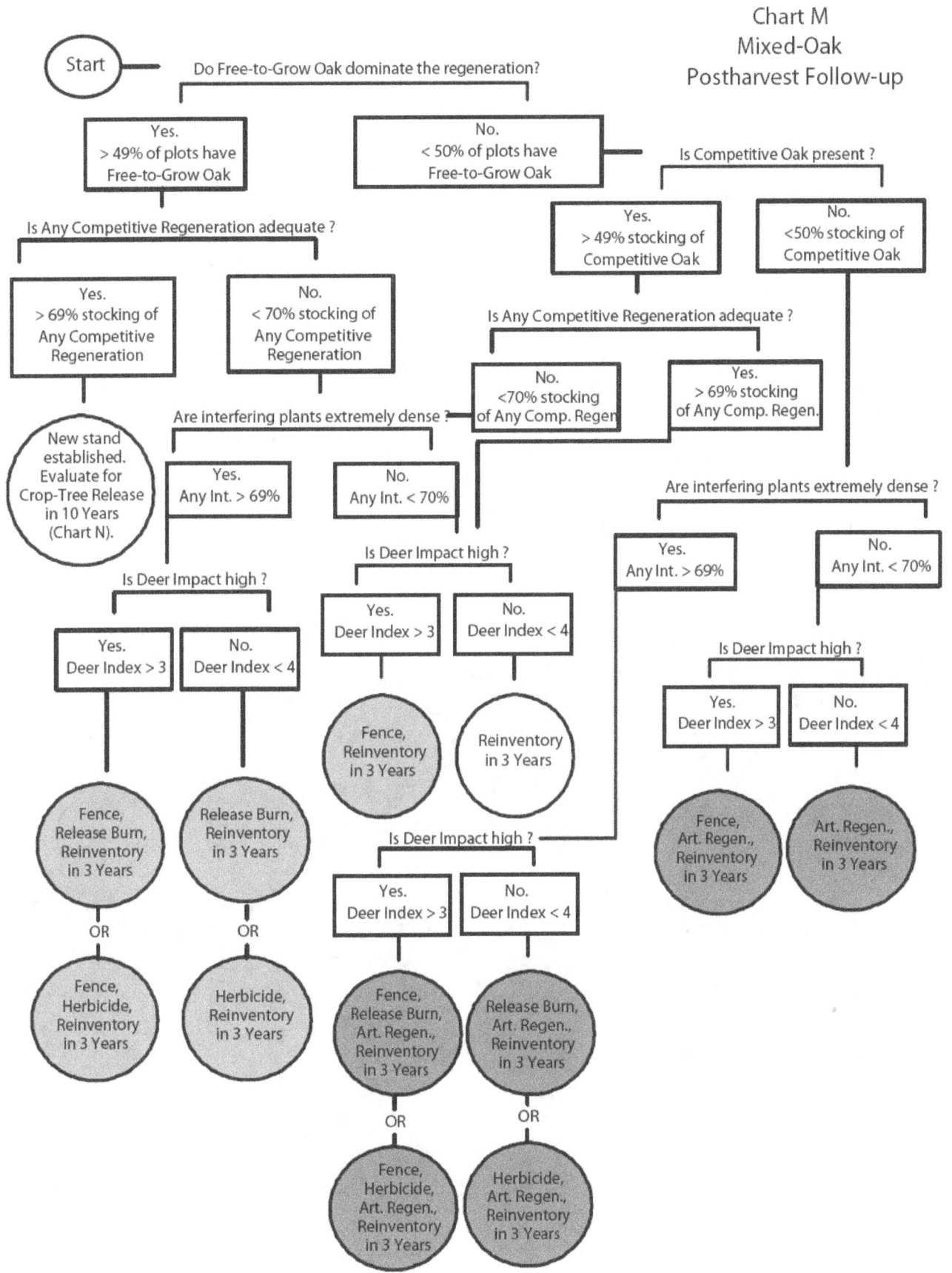

Start

Does predicted number of overstory oaks without CTR (Appendix 7)
meet oak stocking goals at stand maturity (Table 6.2)?

No

Yes

Does predicted number of overstory oaks with CTR
exceed the predicted number of overstory oaks without
CTR by at least 10 trees per acre (Appendix 7) ?

No need to
apply CTR.
Reexamine
in 10 years.

No

Yes

Limited benefit
to CTR.
Reexamine
in 10 years.

Apply CTR to
all oak crop trees
and crop trees of
other desired species
Reexamine
in 10 years.

## ACKNOWLEDGMENTS

The authors are indebted to the leadership and staff foresters of the Pennsylvania Department of Conservation and Natural Resources, Bureau of Forestry for their financial and technical support and unending collaboration of the SILVAH-oak project, the oak ecology and silviculture training course, and this guidebook. Without this support, this project never would have occurred. Within that organization, special thanks are due to Gary Frank, Gary Gilmore, John Hecker, Pete Johnson, Nicholas Lylo, Mark Deibler, and Gary Rutherford. These individuals were especially important in the initial development of SILVAH-oak and the development of the training course. The authors also appreciate the permanent and seasonal field staffs of the Irvine and Morgantown Forestry Sciences Laboratories for their expertise and hard work in preparing for the training courses and carrying out the research studies spawned by the development of SILVAH-oak. Finally, the authors thank Elizabeth Brantley, Daniel Dey, Martin Jones, Thomas Schuler, and Jeffrey Ward for helpful reviews that improved clarity of this manuscript.

## LITERATURE CITED

Abrams, M.D. 2003. **Where has all the white oak gone?** BioScience. 53(10): 927-939.

Abrams, M.D.; Nowacki, G.J. 1992. **Historical variation in fire, oak recruitment, and post-logging accelerated succession in central Pennsylvania.** Bulletin of the Torrey Botanical Club. 119(1): 19-28.

Auchmoody, L.R.; Smith, H.C. 1993. **Survival of acorns after fall burning.** Res. Pap. NE-678. Radnor, PA: U.S. Department of Agriculture, Forest Service, Northeastern Forest Experiment Station. 5 p.

Brose, P.H. 2007. **Development of interim oak assessment guidelines for the SILVAH decision-support system.** In: Buckley, D.S.; Clatterbuck, W.K., eds. Proceedings of the fifteenth central hardwood forest conference. Gen. Tech. Rep. SRS-101. Asheville, NC: U.S. Department of Agriculture, Forest Service, Southern Research Station: 37-45.

Brose, P.H. 2008. **Root development of acorn-origin oak seedlings in shelterwood stands on the Appalachian Plateau of northern Pennsylvania: 4-year results.** Forest Ecology and Management. 255: 3374-3381.

Brose, P.H.; Van Lear, D.H. 1998. **Responses of hardwood advance regeneration to seasonal prescribed fires in oak dominated shelterwood stands.** Canadian Journal of Forest Research. 28: 331-339.

Brose, P.H.; Van Lear, D.H. 2004. **Survival of hardwood regeneration during prescribed fires: the importance of root development and root collar location.** In: Spetich, M.A., ed. Upland oak ecology symposium: history, current conditions, and sustainability. Gen. Tech. Rep. SRS-73. Asheville, NC: U.S. Department of Agriculture, Forest Service, Southern Research Station: 123-127.

Brose, P.H.; Waldrop, T.A. 2006. **Changes in the disturbance regime of upland yellow pine forests in the southern Appalachian Mountains during the 20th century.** In: Connor, K.F., ed. Proceedings of the 13th biennial southern silviculture research conference. Gen. Tech. Rep. SRS-92. Asheville, NC: U.S. Department of Agriculture, Forest Service, Southern Research Station: 467-470.

Brose, P.H.; Van Lear, D.H.; Cooper, R. 1999a. **Using shelterwood harvests and prescribed fire to regenerate oak stands on productive upland sites.** Forest Ecology and Management. 113(2): 125-141.

Brose, P.H.; Van Lear, D.H.; Keyser, P.D. 1999b. **A shelterwood-burn technique for regenerating productive upland oak sites in the Piedmont region.** Southern Journal of Applied Forestry. 23(3): 158-163.

Brose, P.H.; Schuler, T.M.; Van Lear, D.H.; Berst, J. 2001. **Bringing fire back: the changing regimes of the Appalachian mixed-oak forests.** Journal of Forestry. 99(11): 30-35.

Cohen, D.; Dellinger, R. 2006. **Re-examining the role of lightning in the landscape.** Fire Management Notes. 66(4): 25-27.

Cohen, D.; Dellinger, R.; Klein, R.; Buchanan, E. 2007. **Patterns of lightning-caused fires at Great Smoky Mountains National Park.** Fire Ecology. 3(2): 68-82.

Deen, R.T.; Hodges, J.D.; Janzen, G.C. 1993. **The influence of midstory-understroy control treatments on regeneration of red oak species foloowing clearcutting.** In: Brissette, J., ed. Proceedings of the seventh biennial southern silviculture research conference. Gen. Tech. Rep. SO-93. New Orleans, LA: U.S. Department of Agriculture, Forest Service, Southern Forest Experiment Station: 117-121.

Denevan, W.M. 1992. **The pristine myth: the landscape of the Americas in 1492.** Annals of the Association of American Geographers. 82(3): 369-385.

Dey, D.C.; Jacobs, D.; McNabb, K.; Miller, G.W.; Baldwin, V.; Foster, G. 2008. **Artificial regeneration of major oak (*Quercus*) species of the eastern United States—a review of the literature.** Forest Science. 54(1): 77-106.

Ellsworth, J.W.; McComb, B.C. 2003. **Potential effects of passenger pigeon flocks on the structure and composition of presettlement forests of eastern North America.** Conservation Biology. 17(6): 1548-1558.

Fralish, J.S. 2004. **The keystone role of oak and hickory in the central hardwood forest.** In: Spetich, M.A., ed. Upland oak ecology symposium: history, current conditions, and sustainability. Gen. Tech. Rep. SRS-73. Asheville, NC: U.S. Department of Agriculture, Forest Service, Southern Research Station: 78-87.

Gingrich, S.F. 1967. **Measuring and evaluating stocking and stand density in upland hardwood forests of the Central States.** Forest Science. 13: 38-53.

Godfrey, C.L.; Needham, K.; Vaughan, M.R.; Vashon, J.C.; Martin, D.D.; Blank, G.T. 2000. **A technique for and risk associated with entering tree dens used by black bears.** Wildlife Society Bulletin. 28: 131-140.

Grisez, T.J.; Peace, M.R. 1973. **Requirements for advance reproduction in Allegheny hardwoods—an interim guide.** Res. Note NE-180. Upper Darby, PA: U.S. Department of Agriculture, Forest Service, Northeastern Forest Experiment Station. 5 p.

Hanks, L.F.; Gammon, G.L.; Brisbin, R.L.; Rast, E.D. 1980. **Hardwood log grades and lumber grade yields for factory lumber logs.** Res. Pap. NE-468. Broomall, PA: U.S. Department of Agriculture, Forest Service, Northeastern Forest Experiment Station. 92 p.

Healy, W.M.; Lewis, A.M.; Boose, E.F. 1999. **Variation of red oak acorn production.** Forest Ecology and Management. 116: 1-11.

Horsley, S.B. 1981. **Control of herbaceous weeds in Allegheny hardwood stands with herbicides.** Weed Science. 29: 655-662.

Horsley, S.B. 1988. **Control of understory vegetation in Allegheny hardwood stands with Oust.** Northern Journal of Applied Forestry. 6: 261-262.

Horsley, S.B. 1990. **Control of grass and sedge in Allegheny hardwood stands with Roundup-residual herbicide tank mixes.** Northern Journal of Applied Forestry. 7: 124-129.

Horsley, S.B. 1991. **Using Roundup and Oust to control interfering understories in Allegheny hardwood stands.** In: McCormick, L.H.; Gottschalk, K.W., eds. Proceedings of the eighth central hardwoods forest conference. Gen. Tech. Rep. NE-148. Radnor, PA: U.S. Department of Agriculture, Forest Service, Northeastern Forest Experiment Station: 281-290.

Horsley, S.B.; McCormick, L.H.; Groninger, J.W. 1992. **Effects of timing of Oust application on survival of hardwood seedlings.** Northern Journal of Applied Forestry. 9: 22-27.

Hutchinson, T.F. 2006. **Fire and the herbaceous layer in eastern oak forests.** In: Dickinson, M.B., ed. Fire in eastern oak forests: delivering science to land managers. Gen. Tech. Rep. NRS-P-1. Newtown Square, PA: U.S. Department of Agriculture, Forest Service, Northern Research Station: 136-149.

Jacobson, M.; Finley, J.C. 2007. **Pennsylvania woodlands timber market report.** Available online at http://www.sfr.psu.edu/TMR/TMR.htm. (Accessed in November 2007).

Johnson, P.S.; Shifley, S.R.; Rogers, R. 2002. **The ecology and silviculture of oaks.** New York: CABI Publishing. 503 p.

Kirkpatrick, R.L.; Pekins, P.J. 2002. **Nutritional value of acorns for wildlife.** In: McShea, W.J.; Healy, W.M., eds., Oak forest ecosystems: ecology and management for wildlife. Baltimore, MD: Johns Hopkins University Press: 173-181.

Kochenderfer, J.D.; Kochenderfer, J.N.; Warner, D.A.; Miller, G.W. 2004. **Preharvest manual herbicide treatments for controlling American beech in central West Virginia.** Northern Journal of Applied Forestry. 21(1): 40-49.

Kochenderfer, J.D.; Kochenderfer, J.N.; Miller, G.W. 2006. **Controlling beech root and stump sprouts using the cut-stump treatment.** Northern Journal of Applied Forestry. 23(3): 155-165.

Kolb, T.E.; Steiner, K.C.; McCormick, L.H.; Bowersox, T.W. 1990. **Growth response of northern red oak and yellow-poplar seedlings to light, soil moisture, and nutrients in relation to ecological strategy.** Forest Ecology and Management. 38: 65-78.

Lamson, N.I. 1987. **D.b.h./crown diameter relationships in mixed Appalachian hardwood stands.** Res. Pap. NE-610. Broomall, PA: U.S. Department of Agriculture, Forest Service, Northeastern Forest Experiment Station. 3 p.

Lamson, N.I.; Smith, H.C. 1978. **Response to crop-tree release: sugar maple, red oak, black cherry, and yellow-poplar in a 9-year-old stand.** Res. Pap. NE-394. Broomall, PA: U.S. Department of Agriculture, Forest Service, Northeastern Forest Experiment Station. 8 p.

Lamson, N.I.; Smith, H.C.; Perkey, A.W.; Brock, S.M. 1990. **Crown release increases growth of crop trees.** Res. Pap. NE-635. Broomall, PA: U.S. Department of Agriculture, Forest Service, Northeastern Forest Experiment Station. 8p.

Loftis, D.L. 1985. **Preharvest herbicide treatment improves regeneration in southern Appalachian hardwoods.** Southern Journal of Applied Forestry. 9: 177-180.

Loftis, D.L., 1990a. **Predicting post-harvest performance of advance red oak reproduction in the southern Appalachians.** Forest Science. 36: 908-916.

Loftis, D.L. 1990b. **A shelterwood method for regenerating red oak in the Southern Appalachians.** Forest Science. 36(4): 917-929.

Loftis, D.L. 2004. **Upland oak regeneration and management.** In: Spetich, MA., ed. Upland oak ecology symposium: history, current conditions, and sustainability. Gen. Tech. Rep. SRS-73. Asheville, NC: U.S. Department of Agriculture, Forest Service, Southern Research Station: 163-167.

Loomis, R.M. 1974. **Some forest floor fuelbed characteristics of black oak stands in southeast Missouri.** Res. Note NC-162. St Paul, MN: U.S. Department of Agriculture, Forest Service, North Central Forest Experiment Station. 4 p.

Loomis, R.M. 1975. **Annual changes in forest floor weights under a southeast Missouri oak stand.** Res. Note NC-184. St Paul, MN: U.S. Department of Agriculture, Forest Service, North Central Forest Experiment Station. 3 p.

Lorimer, C.G. 1993. **Causes of the oak regeneration problem.** In: Loftis, D.L.; McGee, C.E., eds. Oak regeneration: serious problems, practical solutions. Gen. Tech. Rep. SE-84. Asheville, NC: U.S. Department of Agriculture, Forest Service, Southeastern Forest Experiment Station: 14-39.

Lorimer, C.G.; Chapman, J.W.; Lambert, W.D., 1994. **Tall understory vegetation as a factor in the poor development of oak seedlings beneath mature stands.** Journal of Ecology. 82: 227-237.

Marquis, D.A. 1977. **Devices to protect seedlings from deer browsing.** Res. Note NE-243. Broomall, PA: U.S. Department of Agriculture, Forest Service, Northeastern Forest Experiment Station. 7 p.

Marquis, D.A.; Bjorkbom, J.C. 1982. **Guidelines for evaluating regeneration before and after clearcutting Allegheny hardwoods.** Res. Note NE-307. Broomall, PA: U.S. Department of Agriculture, Forest Service, Northeastern Forest Experiment Station. 4 p.

Marquis, D.A.; Ernst, R.L. 1991. **The effects of stand structure after thinning on growth of an Allegheny hardwood stand.** Forest Science. 37(4): 1182-1200.

Marquis, D.A.; Grisez, T.J. 1978. **The effect of deer exclosures on the recovery of vegetation in failed clearcuts on the Allegheny Plateau.** Res. Note NE-270. Broomall, PA: U.S. Department of Agriculture, Forest Service, Northeastern Forest Experiment Station. 5 p.

Marquis, D.A.; Ernst, R.L.; Stout, S.L. 1992. **Prescribing silvicultural treatments in hardwood stands of the Alleghenies (revised).** Gen. Tech. Rep. NE-96. Radnor, PA: U.S. Department of Agriculture, Forest Service, Northeastern Forest Experiment Station. 101 p.

Marquis, D.A.; Grisez, T.J.; Bjorkbom, J.C.; Roach, B.A. 1975. **Interim guide to regeneration of Allegheny hardwoods.** Gen. Tech. Rep. NE-19. Broomall, PA: U.S. Department of Agriculture, Forest Service, Northeastern Forest Experiment Station. 14 p.

McGill, D.W.; Rogers, R.; Martin, A.J.; Johnson, P.S. 1999. **Measuring stocking in northern red oak stands in Wisconsin.** Northern Journal of Applied Forestry. 16: 144-150.

McShea, W. J. 2000. **The influence of acorn crops on annual variation in rodent and bird populations.** Ecology. 81: 228-238.

McShea, W. J.; Healy, W.M., eds. 2002. **Oak forest ecosystems: ecology and management for wildlife.** Baltimore, MD: Johns Hopkins University Press. 432 p.

McWilliams, W.H.; Alerich, C.A.; Devlin, D.A.; Lister, A.J.; Lister, T.W.; Sterner, S.L.; Westfall, J.A. 2004. **Annual inventory report for Pennsylvania's forests: results from the first three years.** Resour. Bull. NE-159. Newtown Square, PA: U.S. Department of Agriculture, Forest Service, Northeastern Research Station. 95 p.

Mesavage, C.; Girard, J.W. 1946. **Tables for estimating board foot volume of timber.** Washington, DC: U.S. Department of Agriculture, Forest Service. 94 p.

Miller, G.W. 2000. **Effect of crown growing space on the development of young hardwood crop trees.** Northern Journal of Applied Forestry. 17: 25-35.

Miller, G.W.; Stringer, J.W. 2004. **Effect of crown release on tree grade and DBH growth of white oak sawtimber in eastern Kentucky.** In Yaussy, D.A.; Hix, D.M.; Long, R.P.; Goebel, P.C, eds. Proceedings, 14th central hardwood forest conference. Gen. Tech. Rep. NE-316. Newtown Square, PA: U.S. Department of Agriculture, Forest Service, Northeastern Research Station: 37-44.

Miller, G.W.; Kochenderfer, J.N.; Gottschalk, K.W. 2004a. **Effect of pre-harvest shade control and fencing on northern red oak seedling development in the central Appalachians.** In: Spetich, M.A., ed. Upland oak ecology symposium: history, current conditions, and sustainability. Gen. Tech. Rep. SRS-73. Asheville, NC: U.S. Department of Agriculture, Forest Service, Southern Research Station: 182-189.

Miller, G.W.; Kochenderfer, J.N.; Fekedulega, D.B. 2004b. **Composition and development of reproduction in two-age Appalachian hardwood stands: 20-year results.** In: Sheppard, W.D.; Eskew, L.G. comps. Proceedings of the 2003 National Silviculture Workshop. Proc. RMRS-P-34. Fort Collins, CO: U.S. Department of Agriculture, Forest Service, Rocky Mountain Research Station: 171-181.

Miller, G.W.; Kochenderfer, J.N.; Fekedulega, D.B. 2006. **Influence of individual reserve trees on nearby reproduction in two-aged Appalachian hardwood stands.** Forest Ecology and Management. 224: 241-251.

Miller, G.W.; Stringer, J.W.; Mercker, D.C. 2007. **Technical guide to crop tree release in hardwood forests.** Publ. SREF-FM-011. Knoxville, TN: University of Tennessee Press. Available online at http://www.sref.info/publications/online_pubs 24 p.

Millers, I.; Lachance, D.; Burkman, W.G.; Allen, D.C. 1991. **North American sugar maple decline project: organization and field methods.** Gen. Tech. Rep. NE-154. Radnor, PA: U.S. Department of Agriculture, Forest Service, Northeastern Forest Experiment Station. 26 p.

Mitchell, R.J.; Dwyer, J.P.; Musbach, R.A.; Garrett, H.E.; Cox, G.S.; Kurtz, W.B. 1988. **Crop tree release of a scalet-black oak stand.** Northern Journal of Applied Forestry. 5:96-99.

Nowacki, G.J.; Abrams, M.D. 1992. **Community, edaphic, and historical analysis of mixed oak forests of the Ridge and Valley Province in central Pennsylvania.** Canadian Journal of Forest Research. 22: 790-800.

Oliver, C.D.; Larson, B.C. 1996. **Forest stand dynamics.** New York: John Wiley and Sons, Inc. 520 p.

Patterson, W.A. 2006. **The paleoecology of fire and oaks in eastern forests.** In: Dickinson, M.B., ed. Fire in eastern oak forests: delivering science to land managers. Gen. Tech. Rep. NRS-P-1. Newtown Square, PA: U.S. Department of Agriculture, Forest Service, Northern Research Station: 2-19.

Pelton, M. R. 1989. **The impacts of oak mast on black bears in the southern Appalachians.** In: McGee, C.E., ed., Proceedings of the workshop: southern Appalachian mast management. Knoxville, TN: University of Tennessee: 7-11.

Rast, E.D.; Sonderman, D.L.; Gammon, G.L. 1973. **A guide to hardwood log grading.** Gen. Tech. Rep. NE-1. Broomall, PA: U.S. Department of Agriculture, Forest Service, Northeastern Forest Experiment Station. 32 p.

Rentch, J.S.; Hicks, R.R. 2005. **Canopy disturbance intervals, early growth rates, and canopy accession trends of oak-dominated old-growth forests.** In: Van Sambeek, J.W.; Dawson, J.O.; Ponder, F.; Loewenstein, E.F.; Fralish, J.S., eds. Proceedings of the 13th central hardwoods forest conference. Gen. Tech. Rep. NC-234. St. Paul, MN: U.S. Department of Agriculture, Forest Service, North Central Research Station: 323-332.

Ristau, T.E.; Horsley, S.B. 1999. **Pin cherry effects on Allegheny hardwood stand development.** Canadian Journal of Forest Research. 29:73-84.

Ristau, T.E.; Horsley, S.B. 2006. **When is pin cherry (*Prunus pensylvanica* L.) a problem in Allegheny hardwoods?** Northern Journal of Applied Forestry. 23(3): 204-210.

Roach, B.A. 1977. **A stocking guide for Allegheny hardwoods and its use in controlling intermediate cuttings.** Res. Pap. NE-373. Broomall, PA: U.S. Department of Agriculture, Forest Service, Northeastern Forest Experiment Station. 30 p.

Roach, B.A.; Gingrich, S.F. 1968. **Even-aged silviculture for upland central hardwoods.** Agric. Handb. 355. Washington, DC: U.S. Department of Agriculture. 39 p.

Rodewald, A.D. 2003. **Decline of oak forests and implications for forest wildlife conservation.** Natural Areas Journal. 23: 368-371.

Rodewald, A.D.; Abrams, M.D. 2002. **Floristics and avian community structure: implications for regional changes in eastern forest composition.** Forest Science. 48: 267-272.

Rubbo, M.J.; Kiesecker, J.M. 2004. **Leaf litter composition and community structure: translating regional species changes into local dynamics.** Ecology. 85(9): 2519-2525.

Ruffner, C.M.; Abrams, M.D. 1998. **Lightning strikes and resultant fires from archival (1912-1917) and current (1960-1997) information in Pennsylvania.** Journal of the Torrey Botanical Club. 125(3): 249-252.

Sander, I.L.; Clark, F.B. 1971. **Reproduction of upland hardwood forests in the Central States.** Agric. Handb. 405. Washington, DC: U.S. Department of Agriculture. 25 p.

Sander, I.L.; Johnson, P.S.; Rogers, R. 1984. **Evaluating oak advance reproduction in the Missouri Ozarks.** Res. Rep. NC-251. St Paul, MN: U.S. Department of Agriculture, Forest Service, North Central Forest Experiment Station. 16 p.

Sander, I.L.; Johnson, P.S.; Watt, R.F. 1976. **A guide for evaluating the adequacy of oak advance reproduction.** Gen. Tech. Rep. NC-23. St Paul, MN: U.S. Department of Agriculture, Forest Service, North Central Forest Experiment Station. 7 p.

Schlesinger, R.C. 1978. **Increased growth of released white oak poles continues through two decades.** Journal of Forestry. 76: 726-727.

Schuler, T.M. 2006. **Crop tree release improves competitiveness of northern red oak growing in association with black cherry.** Northern Journal of Applied Forestry. 23: 77-82.

Schuler, T.M.; Brose, P.H.; White, R.L. 2005. **Residual overstory density affects survival and growth of sheltered oak seedlings on the Allegheny Plateau.** Res. Pap. NE-728. Newtown Square, PA: U.S. Department of Agriculture, Forest Service, Northeastern Research Station. 9 p.

Shigo, A.L. 1984. **Compartmentalization: a conceptual framework for understanding how trees grow and defend themselves.** Annual Review of Phytopathology. 22: 189-214.

Smith, D.W. 2006. **Why sustain oak forests?** In: Dickinson, M.B., ed. Fire in eastern oak forests: delivering science to land managers. Gen. Tech. Rep. NRS-P-1. Newtown Square, PA: U.S. Department of Agriculture, Forest Service, Northern Research Station: 62-71.

Sonderman, D.L. 1986. **Changes in stem quality on young thinned hardwoods.** Res. Pap. NE-576. Broomall, PA: U.S. Department of Agriculture, Forest Service, Northeastern Research Station. 9 p.

Steiner, K.C.; Finley, J.C.; Gould, P.J.; Fei, S.; McDill, M. 2008. **Oak regeneration guidelines for the Central Appalachians.** Northern Journal of Applied Forestry. 25(1) 5-16.

Stout, S.L.; Nyland, R.D. 1986. **Role of species composition in relative density measurement in Allegheny hardwoods.** Canadian Journal of Forest Research. 16: 574-579.

Stout, S.L.; Marquis, D.A.; Ernst, R.L. 1987. **A relative density measure for mixed species stands.** Journal of Forestry. 85(6): 45-47.

Stout, S.L.; Brose, P.H.; Gottschalk, K.W.; Miller, G.W.; Knopp, P.; Rutherford, G.; Deibler, M.; Frank, G.; Gilmore, G. 2007. **SILVAH-OAK: Ensuring adoption by engaging users in the full cycle of forest research.** In: Miner, C.; Jacobs, R.; Dykstra, D.; Bittner, R., eds. Proceedings of the international conference on transfer of forest science knowledge and technology. Gen. Tech. Rep. PNW-726. Portland, OR: U.S. Department of Agriculture, Forest Service, Pacific Northwest Research Station: 229-238.

Ward, J.S. 1995. **Intensity of precommercial crop-tree release increases diameter and crown growth in upland hardwoods.** In: Gottschalk, K.W., Fosbroke, S.L.C., eds. Proceedings of the tenth central hardwood forest conference. Gen. Tech. Rep. NE-197. Radnor, PA: U.S. Department of Agriculture, Forest Service, Northeastern Forest Experiment Station: 388-398.

Ward, J.S.; Stephens, G.R. 1994. **Crown class transition rates of maturing northern red oak.** Forest Science. 40: 221-237.

Wendel, G.W.; Lamson, N.I. 1987. **Effects of herbicide release on the growth of 8- to 12-year-old hardwood trees.** Res. Pap. NE-394. Broomall, PA: U.S. Department of Agriculture, Forest Service, Northeastern Forest Experiment Station. 4 p.

Wentworth, J. M.; Johnson, A.S.; Hale, P.E.; Kammermeyer, K.E. 1992. **Relationships of acorn abundance and deer herd characteristics in the Southern Appalachians.** Southern Journal of Applied Forestry. 16:5-8.

Whitney, G.G.; DeCant, J.P. 2003. **Physical and historical determinants of the pre- and post-settlement forests of northwestern Pennsylvania.** Canadian Journal of Forest Research. 33: 1683-1697.

Wiant, H.V. 1986. **Formulas for Mesavage and Girard volume tables.** Northern Journal of Applied Forestry. 3(3): 124.

Wiant, H.V.; Yandle, D.O. 1984. **Predicting hardwood height, diameter, and volume.** Northern Journal of Applied Forestry. 1(2): 24-25.

Widmann, R.H.; McWilliams, W.H. 2006. **Changes in the oak resource in the Mid-Atlantic states (DE, MD, NJ, PA, and WV) using Forest Inventory and Analysis data.** In: Proceedings of the Society of American Foresters National Convention. Bethesda, MD: Society of American Foresters.

Zazcek, J.J.; Harding, J.; Welfley, J. 1997. **Impact of soil scarification on the composition of regeneration and species diversity in an oak shelterwood.** In: Pallardy, S.G.; Cecich, R.A.; Garrett, H.G.; Johnson, J.S., eds. Proceedings of the eleventh central hardwood forest conference. Gen. Tech. Rep. NC-188. St. Paul, MN: U.S. Department of Agriculture, Forest Service, North Central Research Station: 341-349.

# Appendix 1:
## Understory Tally Sheet

| Owner/Agency | | Date | |
|---|---|---|---|
| Forest Name | | | |
| County/District | | | |
| Stand Name | | Site index | |
| Stand Area | | Site species | |
| Stand Age | | Site class | |

Deer impact:   very low    low    moderate    high    very high

Restrictions on Silvicultural System:
No restrictions   No clearcutting   No even-age   No multi-tree gaps

Prescription Chart:   Allegheny/Northern Hdwd.    Mixed Oak

Start regenerating now?   Yes    No    Yes, if stand is mature

Want to increase oak?   Yes    No    Residuals desired?   Yes    No

Comments

| | Plot Number | | | | | | | | | | |
|---|---|---|---|---|---|---|---|---|---|---|---|
| | Competitive Oak (#) | | | | | | | | | | |
| 6 | Established Oak (#) | | | | | | | | | | |
| f | New Oak (#) | | | | | | | | | | |
| t | Black cherry (#) | | | | | | | | | | |
| | Conifers (#) | | | | | | | | | | |
| p | Yellow-poplar (#) | | | | | | | | | | |
| l | Other Desirable (#) | | | | | | | | | | |
| o | Saplings (spp. cd) | | | | | | | | | | |
| t | Residuals (spp. cd) | | | | | | | | | | |
| | Tall Woody Interf. (cd) | | | | | | | | | | |
| 26 | Low Woody Cover (%) | | | | | | | | | | |
| | Low Woody Interf. (cd) | | | | | | | | | | |
| f | Fern Cover (%) | | | | | | | | | | |
| t | Grass/Sedge Cover (%) | | | | | | | | | | |
| p | Grapevines (#) | | | | | | | | | | |
| l | Site Limits (1-3) | | | | | | | | | | |
| o | NNIS (spp. code) | | | | | | | | | | |
| t | | | | | | | | | | | |

# Appendix 2:
## Overstory Tally Sheet

SILVAH 5.60 07/2008 USDA Forest Service, NRS, Irvine, PA

| Owner/Agency | | Date | |
|---|---|---|---|
| Forest Name | | | |
| County/District | | | |
| Stand Name | | | |
| Stand Area | | Stand Age | |
| Cruise Type: fixed   variable | | Prism Factor:   5   10   20 | |
| Plot Size | | D.B.H. Class:   1 inch   2 inch | |

**Comments**

| Plot No. | Species | D.B.H. | Quality | Count | # of 8-Ft Bolts | Grade | Defect | Crown | Wildlife |
|---|---|---|---|---|---|---|---|---|---|
| | | | | | | | | | |
| | | | | | | | | | |
| | | | | | | | | | |
| | | | | | | | | | |
| | | | | | | | | | |
| | | | | | | | | | |
| | | | | | | | | | |
| | | | | | | | | | |
| | | | | | | | | | |
| | | | | | | | | | |
| | | | | | | | | | |
| | | | | | | | | | |
| | | | | | | | | | |
| | | | | | | | | | |
| | | | | | | | | | |
| | | | | | | | | | |
| | | | | | | | | | |
| | | | | | | | | | |

**Appendix 3:**
**SILVAH Printout**

< Jun27, 2008 >

SILVAH V5.60 - SILVICULTURE OF ALLEGHENY HARDWOODS AND OAK

```
FILE: C:\USFS-NRS\SILVAH\uncut06.sil
DEFAULTS FILE: C:\USFS-NRS\SILVAH\SILVAH.DEF
OWNER/AGENCY      -- PA BOF              DATE TALLIED: June 2008
FOREST/PROPERTY   -- Clear Creek SF
COUNTY/DISTRICT   -- Jefferson
COMPT - STAND     -- Uncut              TYPE:   TRANSITION HARDWOOD
ACRES             -- 10.00              SIZE:   MEDIUM SAW
STAND AGE         -- UNKNOWN            DENSITY: 80 TO 95%
SITE              -- 70 FOR CO
```

OVERSTORY CRUISE INFORMATION
----------------------------

Overstory data is from an individual tree tally prism cruise using a 10 factor prism, and with trees tallied by 1 inch dbh classes, heights, and pulp & cull grades only.

Overstory data based on 20 plots;
      0 additional plots needed to reach 15 % of the mean;
      0 additional plots needed to reach 10 % of the mean.

Mean basal area is 116 ± 9 square feet per acre at 90% confidence (7% of mean).

UNDERSTORY CRUISE INFORMATION
-----------------------------

Data on advance regeneration, site limitations, and understory are from an extended regeneration tally using 6-ft radius plots.

Understory data is based on 22 plots.

## Appendix 3:
## SILVAH Printout

```
INFORMATION ON REGENERATION AND SITE - ORIGINAL STAND
--------------------------------------------------------

          SPECIES OR              % OF PLOTS   VALUE
           CATEGORY                 STOCKED
          ----------              ----------   -----


DESIRABLE TREE REGENERATION
---------------------------

    --  FIELD INVENTORY:

        BLACK CHERRY                    0          0   Seedlings/acre
        YELLOW POPLAR                   0          0   Seedlings/acre
        CONIFERS                        0        123   Seedlings/acre
        NEW OAK                        27      15564   Seedlings/acre
        ESTABLISHED OAK                 0        700   Seedlings/acre
        COMPETITIVE OAK                 0          0   Seedlings/acre
        OTHER DESIRABLES               14       8789   Seedlings/acre
        ESTABLISHED DESIRABLES         14       9612   Seedlings/acre
        COMPETITIVE DESIRABLES         14       8911   Seedlings/acre
        TOTAL OAK                      32      16264   Seedlings/acre
        RESIDUALS                      23
        SAPLINGS                        0

    --  SUMMARY VALUES - AMBIENT DEER PRESSURE:

        OAK STUMP SPROUTS               3         33   Sprts/ac expected
        ANY ESTABLISHED REGEN          16
        ANY CMP. REGEN OR RESIDS       30
        ANY COMPETITIVE REGEN          16
        ALL ESTABLISHED OAK             3
        ALL OAK                        34

    --  SELECT SUMMARY VALUES - WITH FENCING/NO DEER PRESSURE:

        OAK STUMP SPROUTS               5
        ANY ESTABLISHED REGEN          55
        ANY CMP. REGEN OR RESIDS       69
        ANY COMPETITIVE REGEN          55
        ALL ESTABLISHED OAK            14
        ALL OAK                        60


 ** Summary regeneration stocking values reflect the contribution of oak stump
    sprouts which contribute no more than 20% of total stocking.
```

## Appendix 3:
## SILVAH Printout


```
FACTORS AFFECTING REGENERATION DIFFICULTY
-------------------------------------------

        DEER IMPACT                 3       MODERATE
        SEED SUPPLY                 2       Moderate seed supply

INTERFERING UNDERSTORY
----------------------

        TALL WOODY INTERFERENCE     70**
        LOW WOODY INTERFERENCE      73      51  Plot average
        FERNS                        5       2  Plot average
        GRASSES                      0       1  Plot average
        ANY INTERFERENCE            86
        GRAPEVINES                   5       1  Vines/acre


WOODY INTERFERENCE FOR REGENERATION
-----------------------------------

        TALL WOODY INTERFERENCE        70**

        DETAILS        # PLOTS    (%)      SPECIES
                          2      9.09       AB
                          2      9.09      TOTAL; All species


        LOW WOODY INTERFERENCE         72.7

        DETAILS        # PLOTS    (%)      SPECIES
                         12     54.55      MTL
                          4     18.18      BLU
                         16     72.73      TOTAL; All species


        UNDESIRABLE SAPLINGS AND POLES   23    sq.ft/ac basal area
```

** SILVAH assigns 70% stocking for tall woody interference if there is at least
   10 sq.ft./acre of undesirable saplings and poles (tallied separately in the
   overstory) and there is less than 70% stocking of tall woody interfering
   species.



```
SITE LIMITATIONS FOR REGENERATION
---------------------------------

        SITE LIMITATIONS               0
```

**Appendix 3:**
**SILVAH Printout**

```
SITE INFORMATION - ORIGINAL STAND
---------------------------------

          COVER TYPE              1    Forest
          SITE CLASS              2    Med. productivity
          SITE SPECIES            CO
          SITE INDEX              70
          REL MERCH HT            0.00
          ELEVATION               1800
          ASPECT                  90
          SLOPE %                 5
          TOPO POSITION           6    Upper flat
          OPERABILITY             1    No limitations
          ACCESSABILITY           2    4-wh road at stand


STRESS FACTORS
--------------
          DEER IMPACT                         3    MODERATE



INFORMATION ON SILVICULTURAL SYSTEMS AND WILDLIFE HABITAT - ORIGINAL STAND
-------------------------------------------------------------------------

SILVICULTURAL SYSTEMS
---------------------

NO RESTRICTIONS(EVEN-AGE W/CLEARCUTTING)
Timber production for maximum yield, with high proportion of shade-intolerant
species.

For this system, the stand value is: Medium



WILDLIFE TREES                          NO./ACRE
--------------                          --------

          POTENTIAL DEN TREES                0.000
          EXISTING DEN TREES                 0.000
          SNAGS WITH POTENTIAL CAVITIES      0.000
          SNAGS WITH EXISTING CAVITIES       0.000
          OTHER STANDING DEAD TREES (Not Snags) 0.000



WATER HABITATS WITHIN THIS STAND INCLUDE:
-----------------------------------------
          Unknown


HABITAT CONDITIONS SURROUNDING THIS STAND
-----------------------------------------
          CLEARCUT ACRES W/I 1 MILE          0.00
          CULTIVATED ACRES W/I 1 MILE        0.00
          OPEN ACRES W/I 1 MILE              0.00
```

## Appendix 3:
## SILVAH Printout

```
          WATER HABITATS W/I 1 MILE INCLUDE:   Unknown


OVERSTORY SUMMARY                        ORIGINAL STAND
---------------------------------------------------------

SPECIES >  ALL SP |   RM   NRO    CO    WO    BO   CUC    SO    AB   SVB   SAS

                      COMPOSITION -- BA, % OF BA, TREES


TOT BA     116.0 |  35.8  28.2  25.8  12.8   5.8   2.0   2.0   1.5   1.2   0.5
SPECIES%   100.  |   31.   24.   22.   11.    5.    2.    2.    1.    1.    0.
# TREES    186.  |  100.   16.   30.   12.    3.    2.    1.    8.   11.    2.

                      QUALITY -- % IN AGS

SAPS        36.  |   50.    0.    0.    0.    0.    0.    0.    0.    0.    0.
POLES       77.  |   84.   33.   85.   71.    0.  100.    0.    0.    0.    0.
SM SAW      92.  |   97.   91.   94.   88.  100.  100.   75.    0.    0.    0.
MED SAW     98.  |  100.   96.  100.  100.  100.  100.  100.    0.    0.    0.
LG SAW      89.  |    0.  100.    0.  100.  100.  100.    0.    0.    0.    0.
ALL SIZE    86.  |   85.   93.   89.   88.  100.  100.   88.    0.    0.    0.

                  DIAMETERS AND AGES -- INCHES, YEARS

DIAM        14.9 |  10.2  20.2  15.0  15.1  19.6  17.0  18.6   8.0   4.8   7.0
DIAM MER    15.5 |  11.1  20.2  15.0  15.1  19.6  17.0  18.6  14.0   6.0   7.0
QUAD DIA    10.7 |   8.1  18.1  12.6  13.7  19.0  14.4  17.9   5.9   4.6   7.0

YRS MAT     14.  |   34.    0.   20.   19.    0.    5.    0.   27.   80.   73.
EFCT AGE    87.  |   56.  101.  100.  101.  131.   85.  124.   93.   40.   47.

                             STRUCTURE

Q FACTOR    1.33 |  1.41  0.98  1.10  1.03  0.00  0.00  0.00  0.00  0.00  0.00

                       RELATIVE DENSITY -- %

REL DEN     88.  |   25.   14.   24.   12.    5.    1.    2.    2.    1.    0.
AGS RDEN    74.  |   20.   13.   22.   11.    5.    1.    2.    0.    0.    0.

                  VOLUMES AND VALUES - INT 1/4" LOG RULE

GTOT CDS    38.4 |  11.0  10.2   8.7   4.6   2.1   0.7   0.7   0.2   0.0   0.1
NTOT CDS    30.6 |   8.8   8.2   7.0   3.7   1.7   0.5   0.6   0.2   0.0   0.0
PULP CDS    15.1 |   4.9   3.6   3.6   1.8   0.7   0.2   0.2   0.1   0.0   0.0
GRS BDFT  11033. | 2542. 3425. 2465. 1256.  713.  294.  241.   96.    0.    0.
NET BDFT   9146. | 1497. 3215. 2151. 1094.  666.  260.  223.   40.    0.    0.
DOLLARS    1781. |   72. 1259.   61.  341.   27.   14.    5.    1.    0.    0.
```

90

## Appendix 3:
## SILVAH Printout

```
SPECIES X DIAMETER                        ORIGINAL STAND
-----------------------------------------------------------
```

BASAL AREA - SQ. FT. PER ACRE

| SPECIES > DIA. | ALL SP | RM | NRO | CO | WO | BO | CUC | SO | AB | SVB | SAS |
|---|---|---|---|---|---|---|---|---|---|---|---|
| 1 | 0.0 | 0.0 | 0.0 | 0.0 | 0.0 | 0.0 | 0.0 | 0.0 | 0.0 | 0.0 | 0.0 |
| 2 | 0.0 | 0.0 | 0.0 | 0.0 | 0.0 | 0.0 | 0.0 | 0.0 | 0.0 | 0.0 | 0.0 |
| 3 | 0.0 | 0.0 | 0.0 | 0.0 | 0.0 | 0.0 | 0.0 | 0.0 | 0.0 | 0.0 | 0.0 |
| 4 | 2.0 | 1.5 | 0.0 | 0.0 | 0.0 | 0.0 | 0.0 | 0.0 | 0.0 | 0.5 | 0.0 |
| 5 | 5.0 | 3.5 | 0.0 | 0.0 | 0.0 | 0.0 | 0.0 | 0.0 | 1.0 | 0.5 | 0.0 |
| 6 | 2.8 | 2.0 | 0.0 | 0.5 | 0.0 | 0.0 | 0.0 | 0.0 | 0.0 | 0.2 | 0.0 |
| 7 | 3.0 | 2.0 | 0.0 | 0.5 | 0.0 | 0.0 | 0.0 | 0.0 | 0.0 | 0.0 | 0.5 |
| 8 | 5.0 | 2.0 | 0.0 | 2.0 | 0.5 | 0.0 | 0.0 | 0.0 | 0.0 | 0.0 | 0.0 |
| 9 | 4.8 | 3.2 | 0.5 | 0.5 | 0.5 | 0.0 | 0.0 | 0.0 | 0.0 | 0.0 | 0.0 |
| 10 | 5.8 | 4.0 | 0.5 | 0.5 | 0.8 | 0.0 | 0.0 | 0.0 | 0.0 | 0.0 | 0.0 |
| 11 | 5.8 | 2.2 | 0.5 | 2.5 | 0.0 | 0.0 | 0.5 | 0.0 | 0.0 | 0.0 | 0.0 |
| 12 | 10.5 | 6.5 | 1.0 | 2.0 | 0.5 | 0.0 | 0.5 | 0.0 | 0.0 | 0.0 | 0.0 |
| 13 | 5.2 | 2.2 | 0.0 | 1.0 | 2.0 | 0.0 | 0.0 | 0.0 | 0.0 | 0.0 | 0.0 |
| 14 | 7.5 | 2.5 | 1.2 | 1.8 | 1.5 | 0.0 | 0.0 | 0.0 | 0.5 | 0.0 | 0.0 |
| 15 | 5.8 | 2.2 | 0.8 | 1.2 | 0.8 | 0.5 | 0.0 | 0.2 | 0.0 | 0.0 | 0.0 |
| 16 | 9.8 | 0.8 | 1.5 | 4.2 | 1.5 | 1.0 | 0.0 | 0.8 | 0.0 | 0.0 | 0.0 |
| 17 | 5.8 | 0.5 | 1.0 | 2.5 | 1.8 | 0.0 | 0.0 | 0.0 | 0.0 | 0.0 | 0.0 |
| 18 | 5.0 | 0.0 | 2.0 | 1.5 | 1.0 | 0.5 | 0.0 | 0.0 | 0.0 | 0.0 | 0.0 |
| 19 | 5.5 | 0.0 | 2.5 | 1.5 | 1.5 | 0.0 | 0.0 | 0.0 | 0.0 | 0.0 | 0.0 |
| 20 | 5.8 | 0.5 | 2.5 | 0.8 | 0.0 | 1.5 | 0.5 | 0.0 | 0.0 | 0.0 | 0.0 |
| 21 | 5.5 | 0.0 | 3.5 | 0.2 | 0.0 | 1.2 | 0.0 | 0.5 | 0.0 | 0.0 | 0.0 |
| 22 | 3.5 | 0.0 | 2.0 | 1.0 | 0.0 | 0.0 | 0.0 | 0.5 | 0.0 | 0.0 | 0.0 |
| 23 | 2.8 | 0.0 | 1.8 | 0.5 | 0.0 | 0.5 | 0.0 | 0.0 | 0.0 | 0.0 | 0.0 |
| 24 | 2.5 | 0.0 | 2.0 | 0.0 | 0.5 | 0.0 | 0.0 | 0.0 | 0.0 | 0.0 | 0.0 |
| 25 | 3.5 | 0.0 | 2.0 | 0.5 | 0.0 | 0.5 | 0.5 | 0.0 | 0.0 | 0.0 | 0.0 |
| 26 | 0.0 | 0.0 | 0.0 | 0.0 | 0.0 | 0.0 | 0.0 | 0.0 | 0.0 | 0.0 | 0.0 |
| 27 | 1.5 | 0.0 | 1.0 | 0.5 | 0.0 | 0.0 | 0.0 | 0.0 | 0.0 | 0.0 | 0.0 |
| 28 | 0.5 | 0.0 | 0.5 | 0.0 | 0.0 | 0.0 | 0.0 | 0.0 | 0.0 | 0.0 | 0.0 |
| 29 | 0.5 | 0.0 | 0.5 | 0.0 | 0.0 | 0.0 | 0.0 | 0.0 | 0.0 | 0.0 | 0.0 |
| 30 | 0.5 | 0.0 | 0.5 | 0.0 | 0.0 | 0.0 | 0.0 | 0.0 | 0.0 | 0.0 | 0.0 |
| 31 | 0.5 | 0.0 | 0.5 | 0.0 | 0.0 | 0.0 | 0.0 | 0.0 | 0.0 | 0.0 | 0.0 |
| TOTAL | 116.0 | 35.8 | 28.2 | 25.8 | 12.8 | 5.8 | 2.0 | 2.0 | 1.5 | 1.2 | 0.5 |
| SPECIES% | 100.0 | 30.8 | 24.4 | 22.2 | 11.0 | 5.0 | 1.7 | 1.7 | 1.3 | 1.1 | 0.4 |

ACCEPTABLE GROWING STOCK ONLY

| | | RM | NRO | CO | WO | BO | CUC | SO | AB | SVB | SAS |
|---|---|---|---|---|---|---|---|---|---|---|---|
| SAPS | 2.5 | 2.5 | 0.0 | 0.0 | 0.0 | 0.0 | 0.0 | 0.0 | 0.0 | 0.0 | 0.0 |
| POLES | 20.8 | 13.0 | 0.5 | 5.5 | 1.2 | 0.0 | 0.5 | 0.0 | 0.0 | 0.0 | 0.0 |
| SM SAW | 41.0 | 14.2 | 5.0 | 12.0 | 7.0 | 1.5 | 0.5 | 0.8 | 0.0 | 0.0 | 0.0 |
| MED SAW | 27.5 | 0.5 | 13.8 | 5.5 | 2.5 | 3.8 | 0.5 | 1.0 | 0.0 | 0.0 | 0.0 |
| LG SAW | 8.5 | 0.0 | 7.0 | 0.0 | 0.5 | 0.5 | 0.5 | 0.0 | 0.0 | 0.0 | 0.0 |
| TOTAL | 100.2 | 30.2 | 26.2 | 23.0 | 11.2 | 5.8 | 2.0 | 1.8 | 0.0 | 0.0 | 0.0 |

## Appendix 3:
## SILVAH Printout


NARRATIVE SUMMARY AND ANALYSIS OF STAND
----------------------------------------

This transition stand is dominated by Red Maple, Red Oak, Chestnut Oak, and White Oak that together comprise 88% of the basal area.

This is a medium sawtimber stand, with average diameter of 14.9 inches.

If this stand is managed under an even-age silvicultural system, the several species groups will mature at markedly different times. The average time to maturity (MDM = 18 inches) is 13 years. Effective stand age is about 87 years.

If this stand is managed under an all-age silvicultural system, the distribution of diameters, proportion of sawtimber, and density of shade-tolerant species make it difficult to apply selection cutting.


Relative stand density is 87% of the average maximum stocking expected in undisturbed stands of similar size and species composition. This density is higher than optimum for best individual tree growth. At this relative density, growth rate of the biggest trees is probably moderate, while growth rate of the medium and smaller-sized trees is probably fair and mortality due to crowding moderate.

Thinning to provide more growing space for the better stems is desirable if it will at least pay the cost of harvesting.

Total growing stock amounts to 116 sq. ft. of basal area per acre. Gross total volume in all trees, to a 4-inch top, is 30.6 cords per acre; if divided into pulpwood and sawtimber, the net merchantable volume is 15.1 cords of pulp wood and 9145.6 board feet of sawtimber Int 1/4"log rule. The total stand value is estimated to be about 1780 dollars per acre.

Trees of acceptable quality for future growing stock provide a fully stocked stand by themselves.

The manager wishes to begin regenerating the stand.

Advance regeneration of all types is scarce; harvest cuttings at this time will not likely result in a satisfactory new stand.

Undesirable understory plants may interfere with development of regeneration. Undesirable plants in this stand include tall woody interference and low woody interference.

## Appendix 3:
## SILVAH Printout

```
******RECOMMENDED TREATMENT:******
PREPARATORY CUT, HERBICIDE, RE-INVENTORY


The stand is less than 15 years to maturity.
The manager wishes to begin regenerating this stand now.

Make a PREPARATORY CUT of a shelterwood system to release the already
established seedlings. Reduce relative density to approximately 70% by removing
suppressed, intermediate, and weak codominant trees of all species.  Then,
follow up in 5 to 10 years to determine the next course of action.

Treat the undesirable understory plants with an application of HERBICIDE during
the appropriate part of the growing season. Please refer to the silvicultural
guide for details about implementing this prescription.

The volumes to be removed are:
    690 bd ft (Int 1/4" log rule) and 3.4 cords.


****** CAUTION *******

This prescription generally produces the desired results, requires an
investment, and usually will yield an economic return at the same time.  If such
investment meets your organization's economic criteria, we recommend it.  If
not, we recommend NO treatment. In the case of regeneration prescriptions,
stands generally will NOT reproduce without the recommended treatment.
```

## Appendix 3:
## SILVAH Printout

```
***** MARKING INSTRUCTIONS *****


LEAVE GUIDES:

Leave 75 well distributed trees per acre that are 6 inches d.b.h. or larger.
These trees should be AGS growing in codominant and dominant crown positions.
Within the size and quality constraints below, favor the best trees wherever
possible.  Try to preserve seed sources of scarce species if they are desired in
the regeneration, and strive for uniform spacing among residuals whenever
possible.

Spacing among these leave trees should average 23 feet.

Leave 90 sq. ft. of basal area per acre using the approximate basal area
distribution below.

        Size class              Basal area (sq. ft.)
        SAPLING =                     7
        POLES =                      10
        SMALL SAW =                  41
        MEDIUM SAW =                 28
        LARGE SAW =                   9


CUT GUIDES:

Reduce relative stand density to 70%.

Remove trees in the size classes shown below.

 Cut 3 out of 5 trees from the pole size class.

 Cut 1 out of 8 trees from the ssaw size class.

 Cut 1 out of 8 trees from the msaw size class.

 Cut 1 out of 8 trees from the lsaw size class.

About 52% of the trees cut will be UGS. This will result in removal of about 71%
of the UGS in this stand and about 100% of the merchantable-size UGS.
```

# Appendix 3:
## SILVAH Printout

```
          ORIGINAL   CUT   RESIDUAL  |     ORIGINAL   CUT   RESIDUAL

          BASAL AREA - SQ FT/A       |     SPECIES COMPOSITION - %

SAPS         7.0     0.0     7.0     | % CUC     2.            2.
POLES       27.0    16.6    10.4     | % RM     31.           28.
SM SAW      44.5     3.5    41.0     | % AB      1.            1.
MED SAW     28.0     0.5    27.5     | % PINE    0.            0.
LG SAW       9.5     1.0     8.5     | % NRO    24.           28.
TOTAL      116.0    21.6    94.4     | % WO     11.           11.
                                     | % CO     22.           21.
                                     | % OO      7.            8.

          NUMBER OF TREES - #/A      |     QUALITY -- % IN AGS

# TREES    186.     49.    137.      | % AGS    86.           95.

          DIAMETERS - IN.            |        AGES - YRS.

DIAM        14.9            15.8     | YRS MAT   14.            7.
DIAM MER    15.5            16.7     | EFCT AGE  87.           94.
QUAD DIA    10.7            11.2     |

          RELATIVE DENSITY - %       |          STRUCTURE

REL DEN     88.            70.       | Q FACTOR  1.3           1.1
AGS RDEN    74.            65.       | WEIB C    0.0           0.0

        BD FT INT 1/4", VALUE/A      |       CORD VOLUME/A

GR. BDFT  11033.   932.  10101.      | TOT CDS   38.4    6.5   31.9
NET BDFT   9146.   687.   8459.      | NET CDS   30.6    5.1   25.5
DOLLARS    1781.    88.   1692.      | PULP CDS  15.1    3.4   11.7

------------------------------ TOTAL STAND ------------------------------
        M BD FT INT 1/4", VALUE      |         CORD VOLUME

GR. MBF   110.3     9.3   101.0      | TOT CDS  384.     65.   319.
NET MBF    91.5     6.9    84.6      | NET CDS  306.     51.   255.
M DOLLAR   17.8     0.9    16.9      | PULP CDS 151.     34.   117.
```

## Appendix 3:
## SILVAH Printout

```
                CENTRAL APPALACHIAN OAK GUIDE - ORIGINAL STAND

PROJECTED STOCKING OF OAK SPECIES IN THE THIRD DECADE AFTER HARVEST
------------------------------------------------------------------

      -- SPROUT-ORIGIN STOCKING:           (%)

         CHESTNUT OAK                        20
         RED OAK/SCARLET OAK                 16
         BLACK OAK                            1
         WHITE OAK                            2
         TOTAL SPROUT-ORIGIN STOCKING        40

      -- SEED-ORIGIN STOCKING:             (%)

         ALL OAK SPECIES                     16

      -- EXPECTED TOTAL OAK STOCKING:       55

****** CAUTION *******
This estimate of oak stocking is based on data collected in the ridge and valley
region of Central Pennsylvania.  Please exercise caution when estimating future
oak stocking in other regions.
```

# Appendix 4:
# Allegheny and Northern Hardwood Postharvest Follow-up Tally Sheet

| Owner/Agency | |
|---|---|
| Forest/Property | |
| County/District | |
| Compartment/Unit | Stand Number |
| Acreage in stand | # of plots |
| Remarks | |

## Instructions

1. Use 6-foot-radius plots at a density of one plot/acre
2. Count stems by species and size class.
3. All Desirable Regeneration is the sum of black cherry and all size classes of other desirable in that plot.
4. All Commercial is the sum of beech, birch, and stump sprouts in that plot.

| Plot Number | | | | | | | | | | |
|---|---|---|---|---|---|---|---|---|---|---|
| Pin cherry > 5 ft tall (#) | | | | | | | | | | |
| Black cherry (#) | | | | | | | | | | |
| Other Desirable (#) | | | | | | | | | | |
| Other Desirable > 3 ft tall (#) | | | | | | | | | | |
| Other Desirable > 5 ft tall (#) | | | | | | | | | | |
| All Desirable Regen. (#) | | | | | | | | | | |
| Beech and Birch > 5 ft tall (#) | | | | | | | | | | |
| Stump sprouts > 5 ft tall (#) | | | | | | | | | | |
| All Commercial > 5 ft tall (#) | | | | | | | | | | |

SILVAH 5.60  07/2008  USDA Forest Service, NRS, Irvine, PA

## Appendix 5:
## Mixed-Oak Postharvest Follow-up Tally Sheet

| Owner/Agency | | Date | |
|---|---|---|---|
| Forest/Property | | | |
| County/District | | | |
| Stand Name | | | |
| Stand Area | | # of plots | |
| Comments | | | |

### Instructions

1. Use 6-foot-radius plots at a density of one plot/acre
2. Count only stems that are at least 3 feet tall.
3. Free-to-Grow Oak is a competitive oak with no adjacent trees that are taller.
4. Any Competitive Regeneration is the sum of the stem counts of al regeneration in that plot.

| Plot Number | | | | | | | | | | | |
|---|---|---|---|---|---|---|---|---|---|---|---|
| Free-to-Grow Oak (#) | | | | | | | | | | | |
| Competitive Oak (#) | | | | | | | | | | | |
| Black cherry (#) | | | | | | | | | | | |
| Conifers (#) | | | | | | | | | | | |
| Yellow-poplar (#) | | | | | | | | | | | |
| Other Desirable (#) | | | | | | | | | | | |
| Any Comp. Regen (#) | | | | | | | | | | | |
| Tall Woody Interf. (#) | | | | | | | | | | | |
| Deer Impact (1-5) | | | | | | | | | | | |

SILVAH 5.60 07/2008 USDA Forest Service, NRS, Irvine, PA

98

# Appendix 6:
# Crop Tree Tally Sheet

## Instructions

1. Use 12-foot-radius plots at a density of one plot/acre
2. Count oak and other desirable stems by species and competitive status (CS). Record species of major interfering trees.
3. Competitive Status codes are:

   CS1 = dominant or strong codominant that does not need released;

   CS2 = codominant not threatened by neighboring trees at this time, but may become so in the future;

   CS3 = weak codominant threatened by neighboring trees at this time;

   CS4 = strong intermediate still capable of respond to release.

| | |
|---|---|
| Owner/Agency | |
| Forest/Property | |
| County/District | |
| Compartment/Unit | Stand Number |
| Acreage in stand | # of plots |
| Comments | |

| Plot Number | | | | | | | | | | |
|---|---|---|---|---|---|---|---|---|---|---|
| Oak, Competitive Status 1 (#) | | | | | | | | | | |
| Oak, Competitive Status 2 (#) | | | | | | | | | | |
| Oak, Competitive Status 3 (#) | | | | | | | | | | |
| Oak, Competitive Status 4 (#) | | | | | | | | | | |
| Other Desirable, CS 1 (#) | | | | | | | | | | |
| Other Desirable, CS 2 (#) | | | | | | | | | | |
| Other Desirable, CS 3 (#) | | | | | | | | | | |
| Other Desirable, CS 4 (#) | | | | | | | | | | |
| Major Interference (# and sp. code) | | | | | | | | | | |

SILVAH 5.60 07/2008 USDA Forest Service, NRS, Irvine, PA

## Appendix 7:
## Crop Tree Calculation Sheet

| Owner/Agency | |
|---|---|
| Forest/Property | |
| County/District | |
| Stand Name | |
| Stand Area | # of plots |
| Comments | |

### Instructions

1. Sum the crop trees from all plots on the Crop Tree Tally Sheet by species group (oak or other desirable) and by competitive status.
2. Divide each sum by the number of plots and multiply the result by 100 to get the average number of crop trees per acre by species group and competitive status.
3. Enter each average into both Count columns and multiply by the probability to get the predicted number of crop trees with and without a crown-touching release.
4. The difference between the two predicted numbers helps to determine if a CTR treatment is needed and worthwhile.

| | With CTR treatment | | | Without CTR treatment | | | |
|---|---|---|---|---|---|---|---|
| | Count | Probability | Predicted Number | Count | Probability | Predicted Number | Difference |
| Oak, Comp. Status 1 (#) | | 0.95 | | | 0.75 | | |
| Oak, Comp. Status 2 (#) | | 0.90 | | | 0.50 | | |
| Oak, Comp. Status 3 (#) | | 0.75 | | | 0.25 | | |
| Oak, Comp. Status 4 (#) | | 0.20 | | | 0.05 | | |
| Other Desirable, CS 1 (#) | | 0.95 | | | 0.75 | | |
| Other Desirable, CS 2 (#) | | 0.90 | | | 0.50 | | |
| Other Desirable, CS 3 (#) | | 0.75 | | | 0.25 | | |
| Other Desirable, CS 4 (#) | | 0.20 | | | 0.05 | | |
| Total | | | | | | | |

SILVAH 5.60  07/2008  USDA Forest Service, NRS, Irvine, PA